Printed in United States of America

Contents

Chapter 1

Microsoft Word 365 for Beginners

Microsoft is a tech giant when it comes to some software creation and development. At a little age, I started hearing of this company and her dominance when it comes to word editor. In fact, one of the major software people pay good attention to when they buy their personal computers is Word. There are other companies that specialize in creation and development of word processing software but that of Microsoft is known globally and commonly used by many computer users.

Google for instance has developed a great Word processing software which they called Google Docs. Irrespective of the beauty in the Google LLC product, people still prefer Microsoft Word. Among the beauty in Google Docs is the ability of the software to save data automatically in Google's cloud. But with the development of Microsoft 365 by Microsoft Corporation, this same feature is integrated into it. With Word 365, you can choose to save any data you entered in the word processing product automatically. I will teach you more on how you can do this later.

Word 365 is designed with some good features which were not available in the older versions of the application. Example, there is something Word 365 can do that Word 2007 cannot do. With Word 365, you can right-click on the image in the application environment and then select the option to save the image in your computer. This property is lacking in Word 2007. Can you see the beauty in using up to date applications on your computer?

Microsoft 365 Explained

Microsoft 365 is the "parent package" that houses Word 365 and other Microsoft basic desktop applications. Microsoft 365 is the Office full package which comprises Word 365, Excel 365, PowerPoint 365, Outlook, file storage app and others. Microsoft 365 is of different classifications. I will explain these classifications and what each of them is made up of.

Accessing Office 365

It is import you know how to access Microsoft 365 which is formally known as Office 365. To access Microsoft 365, kindly visit the link https://www.microsoft.com/en-us/microsoft-365. When you visit the link, you will be landed to the homepage of the application which is shown below:

Fig 1: Accessing Microsoft 365

As you are on the page, you can click on any of the link depending on what problem the package will solve for you. If you want Word 365 for your personal use in your PC, the right option for you is to click the link **For home**. It will show you the contents of Microsoft 365 for home and the amount you are to pay for either monthly or yearly subscription. This will take us to the next subheading which is classification of Microsoft 365.

Classification of Microsoft 365

The Microsoft 365, which contains Word 365, which is my major area of concentration is classified into four major categories. These categories are as follow:

- Microsoft 365 for home

- Microsoft 365 for Business

- Microsoft 365 for enterprise and

- Microsoft 365 for education

Microsoft 365 for home

As the name implies, this Office application is designed for use in the home. If you want to buy Office 365 for your personal use, I recommend this class for you. This is the type I use in my Personal Computer. In fact, this category of Microsoft 365 has the highest number of users. When you click the **For home** link, you will be taken to the link where you will download and install in your computer.

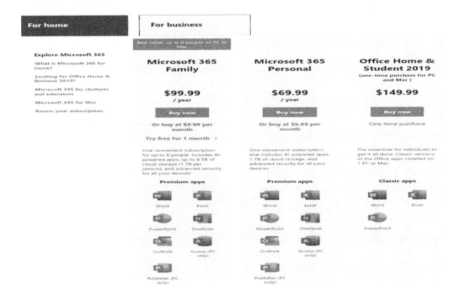

Fig 1.1: Microsoft Office 365 for Home on the web

From the above, you will see that there are some classifications under Microsoft 365 for home. The classifications are **Microsoft 365 Family**, **Microsoft 365 Personal**, **Office Home and Student 2019**. Each of these categories has its own capacity.

5

I specifically make use of the number two in the subcategories, which is Microsoft 365 Personal. So, you can click the **Buy now** link, and follow the step by step guide to install it on your computer, activate and start making use of it.

Microsoft 365 for Business
This is a business package. If you need Microsoft for business, this package is the best for it. In this business package, you can choose to subscribe monthly or yearly. To install Microsoft 365 for business in your computer, just visit the link https://www.microsoft.com/en-us/microsoft-365/business/compare-all-microsoft-365-business-products. When you are on the page, you will see some categories of Microsoft for business, and then buy for your business use. With Microsoft 365, you can chat, call, host online meetings, and collaborate in real time, whether you are working remotely or onsite.

Microsoft 365 for Enterprise
The word 'enterprise' stands for an organization or a business. With enterprise package of Microsoft 365, users can do a lot of things. It comes with many added features. One of the features is the ability to hold meetings with different employees locally and internationally. To have access and start using Microsoft 365 for enterprise, visit the link https://www.microsoft.com/en-us/microsoft-365/compare-microsoft-365-enterprise-plans.

Transform your enterprise with Microsoft 365

Connect and empower every employee, from the office to the Firstline worker, with a Microsoft 365 solution that enhances productivity and drives innovation.

Download the full comparison table	**Microsoft 365 E3**	**Microsoft 365 E5**	**Microsoft 365 F3**
Looking for more? See options for: **Government** **Office 365 for Enterprise**	Get best-in-class productivity apps combined with core security and compliance capabilities for your enterprise.	Get best-in-class productivity apps and advanced security, compliance, voice and analytical capabilities for your enterprise.	**Formerly Microsoft 365 F1** Empower your Firstline workforce with productivity apps and cloud services that allow them to do their best work.
	$32.00 user/month (annual commitment)	**$57.00** user/month (annual commitment)	**$10.00** user/month (annual commitment)
☎ 1 855-270-0615 Available M-F from 6:00AM to 6:00PM Pacific Time ✉ Contact us	Contact sales Learn more ›	Contact sales Learn more ›	Contact sales Learn more › See all Firstline plans ›
✔ Partially included ✔ Included			

Fig 1.2: Microsoft 365 for enterprise subscription plans in picture

From the above screenshot, you can click Contact sales, and follow the step by step instructions to have the app installed in your device and start making effective use of it.

Microsoft 365 for Education

With Microsoft 365 for education, students can keep their data safe. They can complete some assignments effectively and secured without losing any of the data they have stored in Microsoft cloud. This is a welcomed development made possible by Microsoft Corporation. It also makes them to start building their future from today as they get use to know more about technological development and possibilities with this application.

Terms in Word 365 You Need to know

There are some terms in Microsoft Word that I want you to know about. These are terms that I will be using frequently in this teaching. Some readers may know these terms already, but it is not bad to hear them again.

Tab

A tab in this teaching can be defined as a command bar that organizes a software's features at the top of a Word interface. A tab when clicked on will show you other buttons that you can select to perform specific tasks. It is sometimes referred to as ribbon. In addition, tabs of Word 363 consist of groups, which are labelled set of closely related commands.

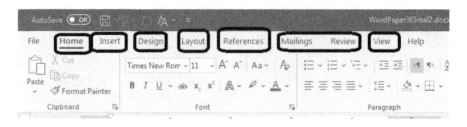

Fig 1.3: Picture shows some of the tabs of Word 365

As shown in the figure above, the functions specified in the rectangular boxes are all tabs of Word 365. But note that they are not all the tabs available in the desktop application as **File** and **Help** are also included. The specified tabs in the figure are **Home**, **Insert**, **Design**, **Layout**, **References**, **Mailings**, **Review**, and **View**.

When you click on any of the tabs, you will be shown the contents. These contents are buttons which you are to click to complete any specific task. When you click the **Home** tab for instance, you will see many buttons which you can select to complete specific tasks. These buttons include bold, underline, italics, text align, case button and so on.

Note: Tabs are also known as Menus.

Button

An application button is an icon which can open app menu of filed related commands. With button, you can open a new document, save an active document, and print and perform other specific tasks in word processing apps. In Word 365, examples of buttons include bold, save, text align, underline, bullet, page numbering button and so on. I will be using specified buttons to complete certain tasks as you progress. You will learn more.

Environment

An environment is a user-defined collection of resources that hosts an application. It is the place where you carry out some tasks on application. If you open blank document of Word 365 for instance, you are landed on the environment. It is on this environment that you start typing your texts and adding other designs like bold, uploading of pictures, graphs, charts and many more.

Cursor

A cursor is a movable indicator on a computer screen identifying the point that will be affected by input from the user. In this book, I will be making use of this term frequently. When you move your mouse, the cursor moves on the screen.

Cursor pointer

This term is used interchangeably with cursor. So, whether I say cursor or cursor pointer, I am referring to the same indicator. The cursor is a pointer that indicates a link, and it is sometimes represented with the image of a pointing hand or a small arrow.

Word

Whenever I use the term 'Word' inside any sentence in this book which starts with capital letter, I mean the major application which this book is all about, **Word 365**. So, take note of that in order not to get confused.

Cut, Copy and Paste

In any Word application like Word 365, you can cut, copy or paste any text or object in the document. When you highlight any text or image in Word document and then right-click your mouse, you will be shown **cut**, **copy** and **paste** among other options.

When you select **cut** among the options, the text or image will be deleted from that area where it is, and you can paste it in another place in the document.

When you select **copy** among the options, the text or image will be copied in the computer clipboard and remains on that area where it is, but you can paste it in another place in the document.

To **paste** means to place the current content of your computer clipboard (the copied text or image) on a part of your document where your cursor is. You can right-click at a spot in your Word document and select any paste options and the data is pasted on that spot.

How to Install and Activate Word 365 in Your Computer

To have Word 365 installed in your computer, you are to first install Microsoft 365. It is from Microsoft Office 365 that you can access Word 365 which is one of the major components of the package. In this section, I will guide you on how to install and activate Microsoft 365 for home. If you want to install for business, it is the same steps you need to take.

To achieve this task, take the following steps:

- Power on your computer and have it strongly connected to internet
- Open your browser in your computer and visit the link https://www.microsoft.com/en-us/microsoft-365

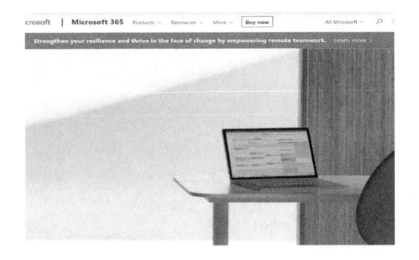

Introducing Microsoft 365

Your productivity cloud across work and life.

For home   For business   For enterprise

For education

Already a customer? Sign in

Fig 1.4: The landing page you will see when you visit https://www.microsoft.com/en-us/microsoft-365 in your browser

- Click **sign in** and sign into your Microsoft account. Please note that you can use your Gmail or outlook account to sign in. If you do not have account with Microsoft before now, you can signup for one and then continue with the installation steps after that.
- Click **For home** so that a new link opens for you to choose the kind of Home package you want to install and use in your computer
- Enter your credit or debit card details to process your payment for the subscription and pay for the duration you want the subscription to last

- On the **Download and install Microsoft 365 Home screen**, select **Install**

- After the download process is completed, select **Run**.

- If the message **"Do you want to allow this app to make changes to your device**? appears, select **Yes**

- Allow the installation process to complete fully. Also, make sure your computer is still connected to internet as the installation process goes on

- Accept terms and condition

- After the installation, in most cases, the applications that make up that Microsoft 365 are automatically pinned at the computer toolbar section.

- Open your Word 365 app after the installation

To open your newly installed Word 365 app, click on it at the toolbar of your computer if it is pinned there by default. If it is not pinned there, just take your cursor to the **start** button of your computer. Type '**Word**' in the search box and the Word app will show up. Just click on it.

- Enter the email address and password you used to open Microsoft account

- The next is that the Word 365 opens. At this point you can choose to create any document of your choice.

These are just the steps on how to install and activate Word 365 in your computer.

Chapter 2

The Home Tab and Completing Basic Tasks

There are some basic tasks you can accomplish through the **Home** tab of Word 365 desktop application. Below is the screenshot showing the tools of the Home tab.

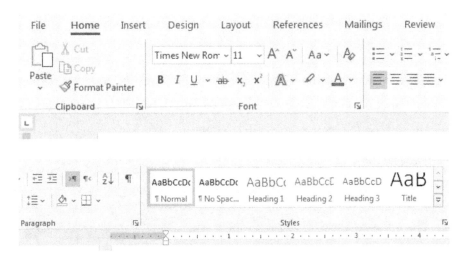

Fig 2: The Home of Word 365 showing different tools

In this chapter, I will teach you how to perform many tasks using the buttons available at the **Home** of Word 365. But before I go into detail, I will like to discuss the **AutoSave** button of Word 365.

The AutoSave of Word 365

Word 365 is developed with AutoSave button. With this button, you can make every data you insert in the word processor to be saved automatically in Microsoft cloud. This information saved in the cloud can be accessed from any part of the world you find yourself tomorrow. For your documents to always be in autosave mode, you have to make sure you save your document file in OneDrive folder.

How to enable AutoSave in Word 365

To enable autosave in Word 365, take the following steps:

- Power on your computer and get it connected to Wi-Fi or mobile data
- Click on Word 365 application which you have already installed in your computer and be patient for it to open

If the Word 365 app is not pinned at the toolbar section of your laptop after installation and activation on your computer, just click the **start** button of your computer and then type "Word" in the search box. The Word 365 app will display on the screen. Then click on the application for it to open.

Fig 2.1: Word 365 pinned at the toolbar section of my pc shown by the arrow

- Click **Blank document** for a new blank document to open

If you want to create from already predesigned templates made available by Microsoft, you can choose any from the many.

14

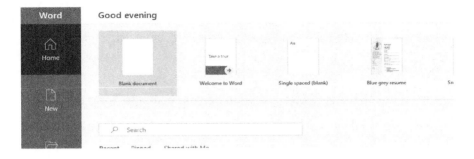

Fig 2.2: Click the **Blank document** for it to open

- Toggle the AutoSave button for it to be turned on and choose to save your document in **OneDrive** folder

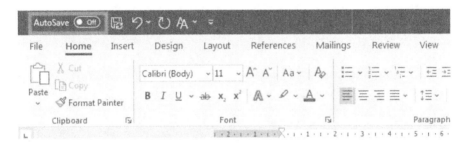

Fig 2.3: The AutoSave section shown above

Depending on how updated the Word 365 desktop app you are using is, if OneDrive app shows up on your Word screen when you toggle the autosave button, click the OneDrive app, type the name you want to use to save the document and click **Ok** button. The document is saved in your OneDrive immediately.

Note: OneDrive may lose memory a times especially when the app is not up to date and also when you do not have strong internet connection. So, ensure everything is in place before saving your document in OneDrive.

Making Texts Bold and Italic

If you want to make texts you typed on Word 365 environment bold, all you are to do are as follow:

- Click the Word 365 application on your computer for it to open
- Type in the texts you want to make bold in the Word environment
- Highlight or select the texts
- Click on the **bold** icon for the texts to be made bold. The bold symbol is shown in the figure below:

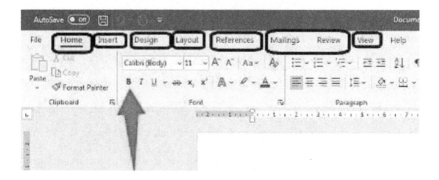

Fig 2.4: The **Bold** symbol of Word 365 shown by the arrow represented by **B**

To make texts you have written already in Word 365 to be in italic, all you have to do is to highlight the texts, and then click the italics symbol represented with *I* as shown below:

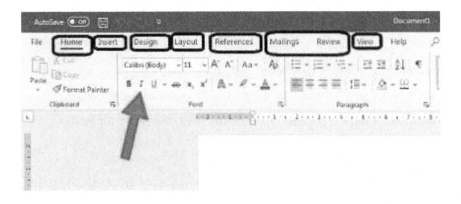

Fig 2.5: The Italics icon shown by the arrow

Note: If you do not know how to highlight texts in Word 365, I will quickly teach you that.

To highlight some texts on your Word 356 environment by dragging method, take the following steps:

- Click your computer's left mouse button at a point close to the texts you want to highlight and keep the button held down
- Drag your mouse pointer across the texts
- When you get to the end of the text you want to highlight, remove you finger from the left button of the mouse you held down.

At this point, your texts are highlighted

Underline, Strikethrough, Subscript and Superscript
Underlining few texts in a document is a way of drawing the attention of a reader of the document to a part of the document. The **Underline** icon is represented with **U** at the toolbar **Home** section of Word 365. You can choose to make your underlined tick or light by choosing from the dropdown of the **Underline** icon.

Subscript button is used to write small letters just below the line of text. This tool is used mainly in Mathematics to differentiate different variables. If you are conversant with Mathematics study and in any way have seen a variable like C_2, know that the "2" was made possible by the use of subscript button/tool. In Word 365 environment, the subscript button is identified as x_2.

Superscript icon is the next after the subscript. Superscript button is used to write small letters just above the line of text. I strongly believe that you went through primary and secondary schools. Do you remember that time when you were taught **Indices**? Do you remember those times your teacher asked the class to give answer to the question 2^4 (pronounced as 2 to power of 4)? That number **4** hanging on the top of **2** is made possible using superscript tool. The superscript icon is represented as x^2 in Word 365.

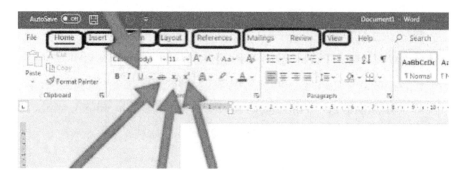

Fig 2.6: Arrow shows Underline, Strikethrough, Subscript, and Superscript respectively

Let me assume that you have opened your Word 365 desktop application, I will then teach you how to apply these explained tools to get the result expected.

- To underline few texts on Word 365, highlight the texts and then click the underline (U) button.

18

- To strikethrough word or letters, just highlight the word and then click the strikethrough button.

- If you want to apply subscript to any text or characters, first write the texts or characters(example C2), then highlight the text or number you want to subscript (in my given example of the two characters, I will highlight only "2"), and finally, click the subscript button. Once you do this, the letter will be below the main letter (example "2" will be below the "C" line).

- To superscript any text contained in another texts, you have to highlight the text which you want to make superscript (Example in texts "K2" I have to highlight 2 because I want to make it superscript). After you have highlighted the letter/text which you want to make superscript, then click the **Superscript** icon. Once you do this, the text is made superscript.

Text Effects and Typography, Text Highlight Color and Font Color

Text Effects and Typography is a button under **Home** tab used to add some flair to text on Word 365 screen by applying a text effect, such as shadow or glow. You can also change typography settings using this button.

Text highlight color button as the name implies is used to mark texts in Word 365 in different color. Please know that this tool is different from font color tool. With text highlight color tool, you can only change the color of that background where the texts are written. Example, the words "smart teaching" has been styled using text highlight color tool. The background of the part where the words were written was changed to green while the texts retained their main color as black.

Font Color as the name implies is the tool on the **Home** of Word 365 which you can click to change the font color of your texts. You can use it to change the text color of words you typed on Word 365 to draw the attention of the reader to a part of the document.

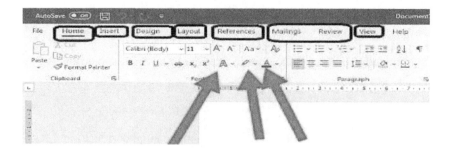

Fig 2.7: Text effects and Typography, Text Highlight color, and Font color tool shown from left to the right by the arrows

Let me assume that you have already opened the Word 365 document, I will teach you how to use these tools practically.

- To apply **Text Effects and Typography** on texts you have typed on Word 365 environment, just select the texts, click the **Text Effects and Typography** icon, select any choice of design from those that will be shown to you. Once that is done, the highlighted texts will change to the design you selected. If you do not like the outcome of the one you selected, you can choose another one until you meet your taste.

- To apply **Text highlight color** on texts, the first thing you are to do is to highlight the texts. The next thing is that you are to click the **Text highlight color** icon, and immediately you will see the effect of the tool on the texts.

- To apply **Font Color** on texts, all you are to do is to highlight the text, click the **Font color** icon and select the color you want the texts or words to be changed to. Example, if I want to Change the font color of the word "WISDOM" to red, I have to follow this guide and at the end choose my color as red. This will give me an end product of the process as WISDOM.

Note: In this teaching, "highlight and select" can mean the same thing, and "tab and menu" can mean the same as well.

Text Alignment
The text alignment tool is one of the major tools used in Microsoft Word application and is under the **Home** tab of Word 365. There are different ways you can align your texts to fit into any part of your document. When I write my book chapters, I usually align the texts to the center and then the body of the document in justify. It makes my work look cool. In few cases, after compilation of my **Table of Contents** of my book, I use left alignment tool on it.

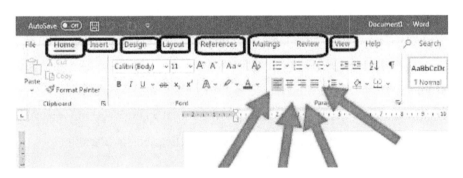

Fig 2.8: Align left, center, align right, and justify tool indicated from left to right

If you are working with Word 365 computer application which was updated between November to December 2020, the **Justify** text styling tool has added options named **Justify, Justify Low, Justify Medium** and **Justify High**.

21

With **Justify,** the text in your document are distributed evenly between the margins of your document. The **Justify Low, Justify Medium** and **Justify High** also justify texts from right to left.

Important Shortcuts on Text Alignment
If you are using Windows computer, the shortcut to align texts towards the left is **Ctrl + L.**

To align texts towards the center in Windows computer, the shortcut is **Ctrl + E.**

If your computer is running the same operating system, the shortcut to align the texts towards the right is **Ctrl + R.**

If you are using Windows computer, the shortcut to Justify texts is **Ctrl + J.**

More Information on Text alignment
To use the shortcuts to align texts in document, you must first of all select the texts and then click any of the text alignment tool you want to apply on the texts. Take for instance I want to align some texts in the chapter 1 of my book using **left align** tool, I am to first highlight the texts and then click **left align** for that to be achieved. If I want to align the entire letters on that document using **Justify** align tool, I will select the entire texts by pressing **Ctrl + A** on my computer keyboard and then click the **Justify** align tool.

Please know that the shortcut **Ctrl + A** implies that you show press the "**Control and the A**" buttons on your computer keyboard at the same time likewise other shortcuts explained.

Line and Paragraph Spacing, Shading and Borders
The Line and paragraph spacing, Shading and Borders tool are the three areas I will discuss in this subheading.

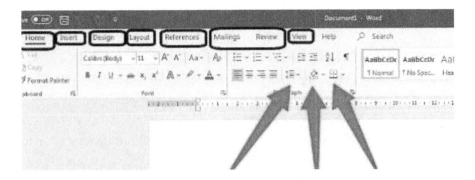

Fig 2.9: The Line and paragraph spacing, Shading and Borders tool shown from left to right by each arrow

With the **Line and paragraph spacing** tool, you can choose the kind of spacing you want to have in your document. It is recommended to use line spacing of 1.5 in words you typed in text editor like Microsoft Word application to make the texts readable. If the texts are clustered, you will hardly read them.

To line-space the words you typed on Word 365, just select the entire words on it, and then click **Line and paragraph spacing** tool, and select the spacing number you want (example 1.5). If you want to choose bigger line and paragraph spacing, you can choose 2.0 or any number of your choice.

Shading tool has similar property with **Text highlight color** tool which I discussed before under a subheading. But there are few things the **Shading** tool can do which **Text highlight color** tool cannot do. You can use **Shading** tool to color the background of cells in a table but **Text highlight color** cannot do it because it is just effective on texts.

To use **Shading** tool on texts or cells of a table, the first thing to do is to select the texts or the cells of the table. After the objects are selected, then click the **Shading** icon and color gallery will be shown to you. Just click on any of the colors you want the texts or cells to be changed to, and the deal is done.

Note: In respect to this study, the term cell means the intersection between a row and a column of table in a document.

Borders tool is used to create and adjust borders in Word document. You can create border around words in a Word document using this tool. Sometimes, putting a border around text will work better in your document than inserting a text box or a one-cell table to achieve a similar look. To add text border around texts, just select the texts first. After that, click the **Borders** tool and select the border design you want.

Further Styling of Texts in Word 365 Document
In this subheading, I will be discussing further styling of texts in Word 365. I will use image to convey my points home for your understanding. Let us get started with this area of interest.

Normal, No Spacing, Heading 1 and 2, Title, Subtitled and Subtitle Emphasis

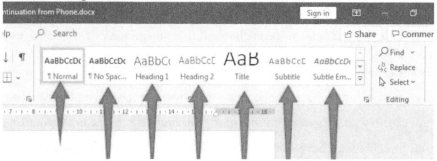

Fig 2.1.1: Normal, No Spacing, Heading 1 and 2, Title, Subtitled and Subtitle Emphasis shown respectively by each arrow

The first tool shown by the left is named **Normal**. This text styling tool is used to style the body contents of texts in Word document. When you type texts in document, the **Normal** text style is selected by default. It is used to construct many text body contents in a document. As the name implies, it is used for normal text.

The second text style shown by the arrow is called **No Spacing**. When you highlight some texts in Word document and then click the **No Spacing** tool, all the line and paragraph spacing you initially set before typing your texts will be lost. As the name implies, this tool is used to disable any form of line and paragraph spacing already established in texts.

The third counting from the left-hand side to the right is known as **Heading 1** tool. This tool is used to style the heading sections of texts in a document for example the chapters and titles of a book. Also, with this, you can make subheadings in a book to be identified as headings. This helps to easily create table of contents and bookmarks automatically in a document. I will teach you on how to create table of contents and bookmarks later.

To apply this tool, highlight the words or drag your cursor to the line of the heading texts, and then click on the **Heading 1** tool. This will make the words change in texts color.

The fourth arrow points at the **Heading 2** tool. When you highlight some texts in a document and then click on this tool, it will make the texts change color (usually blue). But, **Heading 1** text is bigger in text size than **Heading 2** by default. Both Heading 1 and 2 are used to create headings. I use **Heading 1** for chapters and chapter titles of my document and **Heading 2** for my subheadings.

The fifth arrow points at the **Title** tool. You can use the **Title** tool to text-design the main title of your article. Take for instance that this book is just an article with the title "Word 365 for Beginners", if I select this main title texts and then click the **Title** tool, the style of the text will change immediately I select another title style. I will see the title appear as WORD 365 FOR BEGINNERS because I chose that title tool option.

The sixth text style tool stands for **Subtitle**. You can use this Word tool to differentiate between subtitles and other text parts of a document file. To make change with this tool, just select the texts and then click the **Subtitle** tool.

The seventh which is the last when you count from the left-hand side to the right stands for **Subtitle Emphasis** tool. If you want to see the effect of this tool, just select few texts, and then click the **Subtitle Emphasis** tool. You will see the change that will be shown to you.

Ribbon Display Option

In working in Word 365 computer application, there is possibility that you may run into trouble that has to do with ribbon. In this teaching ribbon and tabs mean the same thing. You may mistakenly press somewhere in your computer and the ribbons will be hidden. When this happens, you will find it difficult to complete some tasks because it is ribbon tools that we use to work in Word 365.

The **Ribbon Display Option** tool is located at the top right-hand side of the word screen. It is an arrow that points up close to your Microsoft profile name.

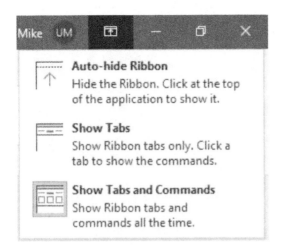

Fig 2.1.2: The **Ribbon Display Option** position

When click that section, always select **Show Tabs and Commands**, so that you can work easily in Word document. Whenever some tabs or command are hidden in your Word application, just click the **Ribbon Display Option** and select **Show Tabs and Commands.**

Chapter 3

Other Basic Tasks in Word 365

When you understand the fundamental areas in any areas of study, it will help you to find it easy in completing the complex areas. That is the reason I am taking my time to explain to you the basic areas in Word 365. In this chapter there are some knowledge you will gain. Without taking much of your time, let's get started.

How to Save Files in Word 365
This area is very important. When **AutoSave** is not enabled by you in Word 365, you are likely to lose the data you typed in your document. As a result of this, you need to know how to save your file in any folder in your laptop to avoid feeling bad because you lost important information you have typed or inserted in the Word document.

In this teaching, I assume that you have opened your Word 365 application, typed and uploaded some objects you want to have in the document. To save your document file, take these steps:

- Click the **File** tab at the top left-hand corner of the Word application

Fig 3: The **File** button shown

- Click **Save As**, which is one of the options that will be shown to you
- Click **Browse** folder or any other section you want to save your file including OneDrive

Fig 3.1: Available options where you can save your document

When you select **Browse**, the system will open, and you are to choose the location you want to save your file. You can choose to save the file in your **Document** folder or any other folder you created by yourself to save a category of files.

- Choose the format you want to save your file and give it name that you can use to easily find it

When you select the location to save the file, the file format may not be **doc** or **docx** by default. Please if you notice that the system selected a format different from doc or docx, just change it unless you specifically want to use the one chosen by the system. The most common format used to save document files are either doc or docx. So, click the dropdown at the **Save as type** line and then select doc or docx before giving that file a name.

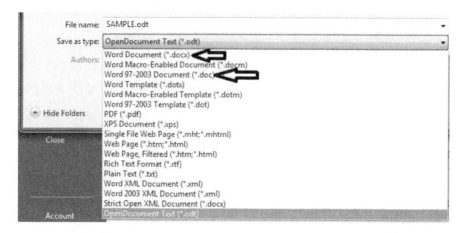

Fig 3.2: Choose doc or docx document format as shown by the arrow

Giving your file name is of good importance because it can help you to easily find the file when you forget the location you initially saved it. You can just type the name or few letters among the name you used to save the file in your computer search box and search, and within a short time the file becomes sorted out among others. Once you give your file the name you want it to bear, click the **Save** button and it is saved.

In addition, if you go back to your Word document environment to keep typing and uploading other objects, you can easily save your data. If you are working using Windows computer, you use the shortcut **Ctrl + S** to save the file without given it any other name.

Font, Font Size, Increase and Decrease Font Size Tools

This is a new subheading where I will teach you another basic information in Word 365 desktop application. The font you choose before typing in Microsoft Word document determines how the texts will look like. Microsoft during the development of this their word processing app integrated many kinds of font into it. One of the reasons for that is to meet the demand of different people who use the application for different purposes. For example, most times when I type texts for my book, I use the font called Times New Roman. Why I do so is because this font is best for me in formal textbooks. But you do not expect an artist to use such when making some artistic writings. He has to choose the one that fits the job he does. Microsoft is wise and they did everything within their power and made sure they integrated different fonts for different designs. Before I forget, the term "font" means a graphical representation of text that may include a different typeface, point size, weight, color, or design.

Font size controls how big or small a font will be. Font size is determined by number. If you choose a font size of 10 and later choose font size of 14, you will see that 14 is bigger than 10 by size. If you are writing the body part of any document, it is recommended you choose font size from number 11 to number 14. But if you are writing for academic or legal purpose, you are to stick to the font size you are instructed to use. In addition, most book chapters are written with font sizes from 16 to 18.

Increase Font Size button is a feature added by Microsoft, which is the company that developed Word 365, to add beauty to the application document. The fact is that you can do without this tool because **Font size** tool can do the same thing that **Increase Font Size** can do. With this tool, you can just increase the font size of the texts typed in document.

Decrease Font Size just as the name sounds is used to decrease text size. If the size of the texts you are working with is 14 for example, you can use this tool to reduce it to size 13, 12, 11 or any possible size you want. Notwithstanding that Microsoft Inc. added this tool in Word 365, Font size tool can still do the same job it does.

Practical Application of Font, Font Size, Increase and Decrease Font Size Tools

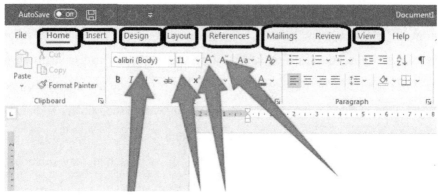

Fig 3.3: Font, Font Size, Increase Font Size and Decrease Font Size Buttons respectively pointed by the arrow from left to right

I will guide you through on how to practically apply these tools to make changes in the texts you have in Word 365 document.

How to Choose Font

In most cases, when you open your Word 365, the default font you see is **Calibri (Body)**. If you want to choose another font different from the one made available by default, take these steps:

- Drag your computer **cursor** to the **Font** and click it

As you click the font tool, you will be shown many font types

- Scroll down the font gallery until you find the one you like. The fonts are usually arranged alphabetically.
- Click on the font you want to use

Once you click on that font you want your texts to be typed in, then start typing your texts in the document. This will make the texts to be in that font you selected.

But if you want to change the font of few words in your document, just take these simple steps:

- Select the few words
- Click the **Font** tool
- Choose the font you want

That is all. The words will immediately change to the one you selected. Just click out in any spot on the Microsoft Word environment and continue with your typing.

How to Choose Font Size

To choose font size that will control the texts you type in Word 365 document, follow this guide:

- Click on the Word 365 app to open and then click the **Font Size** tool which I showed to you in picture
- Select the font size you want by scrolling up or down
- You can also type in the number in the font size box, example '12' and then hit enter key of your computer keyboard

How to Apply Increase Font Size tool

To make changes with the **Increase Font Size** tool when you have already opened Word 365 application and typed texts in it, take these steps:

- Click the **Home** tab

- Select some texts which you want to apply **Increase Font Size** on

- Start clicking on the **Increase Font Size** tool

- The more clicks on the **Increase Font Size**, the bigger the size of the texts

How to Apply the Decrease Font Size tool

I assume that you have typed some texts in your in Word 365 at this stage.

To apply the **Decrease Font Size tool,** take these steps:

- Click the **Home** tab

- Select some texts which you want to apply **Decrease Font Size** on

- Start clicking on the **Decrease Font Size** tool

- The more clicks on the **Decrease Font Size** tool, the smaller the size of the text

Change Case, Clear all formatting and Bullets

These three tools are all found in the toolbar section of Word 365 which are integrated into the **Home** tab.

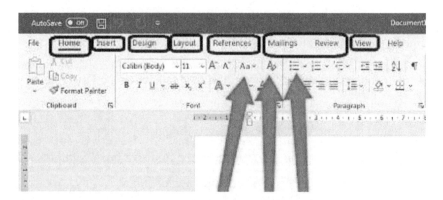

Fig 3.4: **Change Case, Clear all formatting** and **Bullets** shown by each arrow counting from left to right

Counting from the left-hand side to the right, the first arrow points at **Change case** tool, followed by **Clear all formatting** tool, and finally the **Bullets** tool.

The **Change case** tool is used to change the case of texts in the Word app. What it implies is that you can use the **Change case** tool to change texts from capital letters to small letters and vis-à-vis. To achieve this, you can select the texts or word you want to change to capital or small letters, click the **Change case** tool, and then select the case you want the texts to be changed to.

Clear formatting tool is used to clear all features or designs added to texts. It is a tool used to return text to its default state. Take for instance you are writing a chapter of a book, and after typing the texts decide to color-fill each subheadings of the chapter with yellow color. For you to remove the yellow color from the subheadings to return the texts to their default state, you are to use **Clear formatting** tool. To clear format texts which are already in the Word 365 environment, take these steps:

- Select the texts you want to clear format
- Click the **Home** tab of Word 365
- Click the **Clear formatting** tool

The texts will be clear from any text color or the added features on the texts.

Bullets are used to list items on Word 365 environment. It makes list of items or objects appear organized. Bullet can be added to differentiate between the different points you want to make in your document. When you click at the dropdown of the bullet tool, you will see some nice bullet designs made possible by Microsoft. If you want to use bullets to list items in Word 365 when the application has been opened already, do it like this:

- Click empty part of the application environment where you want the bullet to start
- Click the **Home** tab of your Word 365 if not at **Home** already by default
- Click the bullet tool (if you do not know the bullet tool, check the picture I uploaded before now)
- Start typing your texts

When you finished typing the words you want to have in the line of the bullet, tap **Enter key** of your computer and another bullet will be placed the next line. You are to continue your typing and keep following the trend until you are done with the items you want to list.

Numbering, Multilevel list, Decrease Indent and Increase Indent

Numbering, **Multilevel list**, **Decrease** and **Increase indent** are still Word tools found under the **Home** tab. Each of these tools has areas they are best applied to get good result in return.

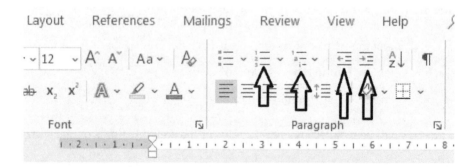

Fig 3.5: **Numbering, Multilevel List, Decrease** and **Increase Indent** shown by arrows counting from left to right

Numbering tool under the **Home** tab is used to list items in Word 365 document. With this tool, you can list items from number 1, 2, 3, 4 and so on. When you click the dropdown at the **Numbering** tool, you will be shown more numbering options. These options include numbering in Roman figure and numbering in alphabetical order. Take for instance I want to number list of items I bought from market like chicken, carrots, oil, beans and rice, I can use the Numbering button to list them in number as 1, 2, 3, 4, and 5.

How to use Numbering Tool
To use the Numbering tool to list items in Word documet, take the following steps:

- Click the Word 365 desktop application for it to open, and click **Blank document** option
- By default, you will be on the **Home** tab but if you are already working under different tab, just click **Home** tab
- Click at a spot in your document where you want to start your listing
- Click the **Numbering** tool
- Start typing your texts of the item you want to list
- When you are done typing one item, hit the enter key of your keyboard for another number to be inserted below the former
- Start typing another item. Follow this trend until you are done with the items you want to list
- When you are done with the last item you want to list, click the **Numbering** tool again for the **Numbering** tool to be disabled

Multilevel List is another tool/button founder under the **Home** tab of Word 365. With this button, you can combine numbers and letters to make list just as seen in some examination questions that has numbers as 1a, 2a, 3a, 4b, 5c and so on. When you click the dropdown at the Multilevel button, you will be shown some other formats of the list you can change to. Also, from the dropdown options, you can customize the Multilevel format you want to use.

You have to click the **Define New Multilevel List...** and complete the rest customization process.

How to use Multilevel Tool

To use the **Multilevel** tool to list items in Word, take the following steps:

- Click the Word 365 desktop application for it to open, and click **Blank document** option
- By default, you will be on the **Home** tab but if you are already working under different tab, just click **Home** tab
- Click at a part of the Word environment where you want to start your listing
- Click the **Multilevel** tool
- Start typing your texts of the item you want to list
- When you are done typing one item, hit the enter key of your keyboard for another **Multilevel** list to be inserted
- Start typing another item. Follow this trend until you are done with the items you want to list
- When you are done with the last item you want to list, click the **Multilevel** tool again for the **Multilevel** list tool to be disabled

With **Decrease** and **Increase Indents,** you can adjust texts in a paragraph to the left- and right-hand side respectively. Note that you can create paragraph in Word document for desktops (computers) by tapping the Enter key of your keyboard and then start typing your texts. So, each time you hit the **Enter** key of your computer, you create new paragraph.

By default, texts typed in Word document are arranged toward the left margin of the application. As a result of this, when you place your cursor pointer at a paragraph and click the **Decrease Indent** button, you will not notice any remarkable difference in the paragraph. But when you click **Increase Indent,** you will notice remarkable change.

How to Apply Increase Indent in Word

I will like to start this guide by showing image that displays typed words in two different paragraphs. Then during the teaching, I will show you how the sentences that make up a paragraph will change when **Increase Indent** tool is applied to the paragraph.

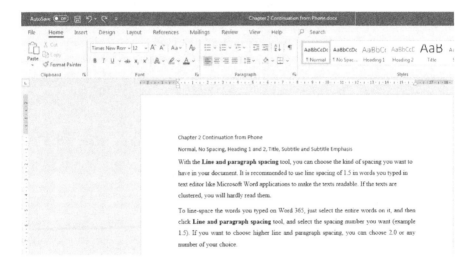

Fig 3.6: The picture showing two different paragraphs before impact of **Increase Indent** on one of the paragraphs

To apply **Increase Indent** in a paragraph, take the following steps:

- Tap the **Word 365** app in your computer to open the application
- Click **Blank document** for it to open blank document
- Click the **Home** tab if not there by default
- Start typing texts in the document, and make paragraphs
- Drag your cursor pointer to one of the paragraphs and click on any spot there

- Click the **Increase Indent** button

The more the number of times you click the **Increase Indent** button, the more the paragraph containing the texts move towards the right-hand side.

Chapter 2 Continuation from Phone

Normal, No Spacing, Heading 1 and 2, Title, Subtitle and Subtitle Emphasis

With the **Line and paragraph spacing** tool, you can choose the kind of spacing you want to have in your document. It is recommended to use line spacing of 1.5 in words you typed in text editor like Microsoft Word applications to make the texts readable. If the texts are clustered, you will hardly read them.

To line-space the words you typed on Word 365, just select the entire words on it, and then click **Line and paragraph spacing** tool, and select the spacing number you want (example 1.5). If you want to choose higher line and paragraph spacing, you can choose 2.0 or any number of your choice.

Fig 3.7: The outcome after I clicked the **Increase Indent** twice when the **Increase Indent** was applied at paragraph 2

The Sort, Show Paragraph Marks and Other Tools

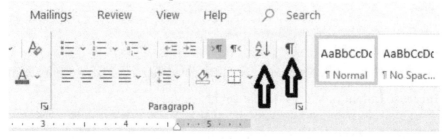

Fig 3.8: The **Sort** and **Show Paragraph Marks and Other hidden formatting symbol** tool from left to right

With **Sort** tool of Word 365, you can sort out items you have listed in Word document in alphabetical or numerical order. You can list from ascending order (that is From **A** to **Z**) or from descending order (from **Z** to **A**). If for instance you have list of items like Salt, carrots, rice, 56 cups of rice, 10 cups of beans and 13 teaspoons of milk, you can arrange them alphabetically or numerically using the **Sort** tool.

Step by Step Guide on How to use Sort Tool in Word 365
To use Sort tool in Word, take these steps:

- Click the Word 365 app for it to open
- Click **Blank document** for it to open blank document
- Select/highlight the list of items you want to sort
- Click the **Home** tab
- Click the **Sort** tool which I showed in the picture above
- Choose how you want to sort the items, and click **Ok** button

You can sort from **Paragraph** to **Number** or any other option. When you sort from Paragraph to number, if the list of the items contain items that start with mixture of different numbers, then the items will be listed from those that start with lesser numbers to higher numbers if **sort by Ascension** is selected.

Show Paragraph Marks and Other hidden formatting Symbol Tool
This is another tool in Word 365 that you can select to show you all the paragraphs and other hidden formatting symbols in Word document. If the documents you are creating are divided into sections, when you click this tool, you will be shown all the sections including the paragraphs that make up the documents.

To Access this **Show paragraph marks and other hidden formatting symbol** tool when you have finished typing and uploading what you want in your document file, take these steps:

- Click the **Home** tab of your Word 365 document

- Click the **Show paragraph marks and other hidden formatting symbol** tool

- Once you do that, all paragraphs and other hidden formatting symbol in the document will be displayed to you.

If you want to exit from **Show paragraph marks and other hidden formatting symbol,** click that same tool and your document will return to normal.

Chapter 4

Completing Some Tasks Through the Insert Tab of Word 365

There are some tasks which you can easily complete through the Insert tab of Word 365 computer application. In this chapter, I will walk you through on them. These are important tasks and believe me, you will be happy you do learn these skills at the end. If after reading through this chapter you find it difficult on how to complete any of these tasks, do not hesitate to write to me through my email which I will leave with you at the end of this book. You bought this book because you want it to help on how to solve some problems, and that I want you to achieve.

Categories in Word 365 Document Insert Tab
To see the categories in **Insert** tab of Word 365, just click your Word 365 application, select **Blank document**, and as the Blank document opens, click **Insert**, which is one of the major tabs on top part of the Word environment.

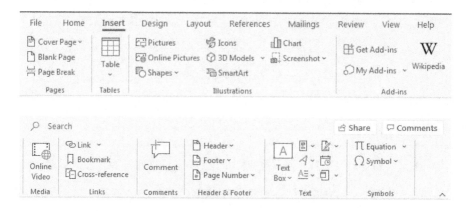

Fig 4: Picture shows the categories in **Insert** tab of Word 365

The categories under the **Insert** tab of Word 365 are as follow:

- Pages
- Tables
- Illustrations
- Add-ins
- Media
- Links
- Comments
- Header & Footer
- Text and
- Symbol

The Pages Category

In Pages category, there is **Cover Page**, **Blank page** and **Page Break**. With Cover Page, you can insert page cover in any document file you are building. Let us assume that you have typed all the texts that make up a textbook that you want to publish on your own, you can click the **Cover Page** button, and choose any cover page of your choice. As of the time of first publication of this book, there were 16 in-built cover page templates made available in Word 365. So, you can click on any of them, and it gets inserted into your Word file. As the cover page is inserted, you can add the title of the document in the space provided, add the name of the author, and other information which is needed in the predesigned cover page.

When you click the **Cover Page** tool. you can also obtain other available covers online from office.com. But before you can do that successfully, your computer needs to be connected to the internet.

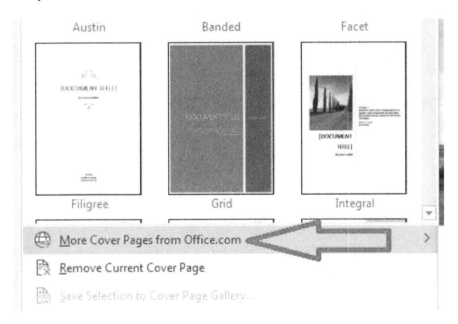

Fig 4.1: Click there to have access to more book covers from office.com

Blank page under **Page** category of **Insert** allows you to quickly insert a new blank page in Word 365 desktop application document. If you just started typing texts in Word 365 environment, and at a point you want the system to take you to a page that is blank in that same document file, just click the **Blank Page** button and your computer cursor will be taken to a new blank page. As you are on that blank page, you can start typing fresh texts. With this tool, you do not need to scroll before you get to a new blank page to continue your typing.

Page Break is another important button under the **Pages** category of **Insert** tab. If you are a writer that writes and publish books independently, **Page Break** is a tool you need to understand. By default, page breaks are inserted in Word 365. In a simpler language, a Page Break is that gap between one page of Word and the other. If you **double-click** between the two gaps, the page break between the two pages will close. When it closes and you double-click at that spot again, the page break is created again. But if you want to insert it manually without double-clicking, then you follow the manual steps through the **File** tab.

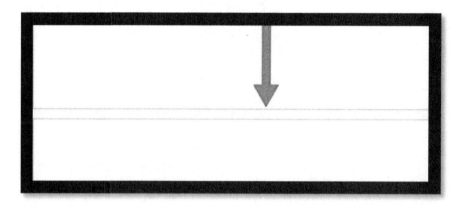

Fig 4.2: A part of Word 365 document where page break is inserted

To manually insert Page Break in Word document, take these steps:

- With your cursor click any spot in your document where you want one page to end and the next to begin.
- Click **Insert** tab and then click **Page Break**.

With these quick steps, you will insert page break at that part of Word document

The Tables Category of Word 365

The **Tables** tool is one of the major divisions in **Insert** tab. Through the **Table** group, you can insert tables in Word 365. Take for instance you want to prepare a statement of account for the company you work for, the two major tools you can use to get this job done is table or spreadsheet. But table is usually the most used tool for the task. When you click **Table** tool under **Insert**, you will see some options on how to insert table in Word.

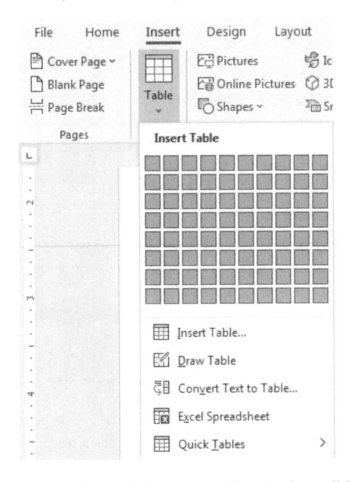

Fig 4.3: When the Table tool was clicked showing available options

From the above screenshot, you can just click on a box for a table to be inserted in your document. Also, you can just click **Insert Table...** and type the number of rows and columns you want to make up your table. The other two options are using **Excel Spreadsheet** or **Quick Tables** option. When you select **Excel Spreadsheet**, a new spreadsheet will be inserted in the Microsoft Word document. You can then start building your table by entering the necessary data. With **Draw Table**, you can draw table that will meet what you want. It is that simple.

Step by Step Guide on How to Insert Table in Word 365
In this section, I will teach you how to insert table in Word 365 without any much stress. To insert table in Word 365document, take the following steps:

- Click the Word 365 app installed on your computer for it to open, and select **Blank document** for it to open
- Click the **Insert** tab at the top part of the Word interface
- Click **Table** button
- Drag your computer cursor to a point in the small boxes representing rows and columns and click at that spot. Once you do that, the table is inserted.
- You can click in any of the cells (the boxes that make up the table) and type in texts you want to have in each cell.

But what happens if the table you inserted contains more rows and columns not as you intended

If after inserting table in Word and you find out the cells are more than what you wanted and wish to reduce them so that it matches the table you need, take the following steps:

- In that table you inserted, click inside any of the cells with your cursor
- Right-click inside the cell

When you right-click in the cell, you will be shown some options

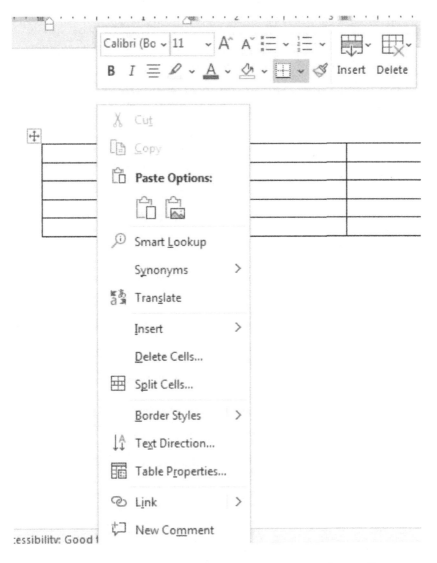

Fig 4.4: The options you will see when you right-click in a cell

- Select **Delete Cells...** among the other options

As you click **Delete Cells...** you will see the popup below

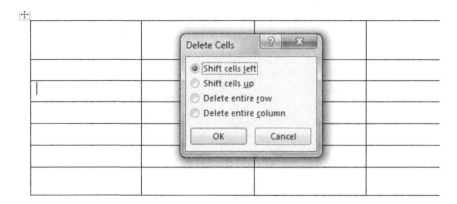

Fig 4.5: What will show up when you select **Delete Cells...**

- Check the option **Delete entire row** or **Delete entire column** depending on what you want to achieve
- Click **OK** button. That is all you are to do to get the job done.

How to Add cells in Table
At this point, I assume that you have already inserted table in Word document. Maybe after inserting you table in Word 365, you discovered you need to add more columns or rows to add to what you had already, to do that, take these steps:

- Click in a cell in the table
- Right-click in that cell to be shown some options
- Select **Insert** among the options

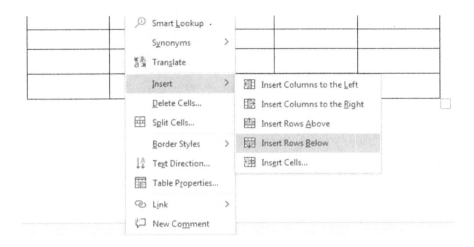

Fig 4.6: Options that will be displayed when you select the **Insert**

- Select whether to insert row or column

If I want to insert rows, I will click **Insert Rows Above** or **Insert Rows Below**. But if I want to insert column, I will select **Insert Columns to the Left** or **Insert Columns to the Right**. Feel free to experiment with the options and see the changes you will experience. If the result you get is not what you expect, go back to your previous state by clicking **Undo** button. So, do not be afraid of trying the options out.

How to Adjust Table Size using your Computer Cursor

When you inserted table in Word 365 and you feel the cells that make up the table are small, you can manually adjust them to the height and size you want them to be. What you are to do is to place your cursor on the line that makes up the row or column of the table, **press and hold your mouse left button**, and then drag towards up, down, left or right direction depending on whether you are adjusting the row or the column of the table.

How to Delete Table in Word 365

You can decide to delete the table you are building in Word 365 and then start afresh. But if you do not know how to do that, that is where the problem comes in. Before I go into how to delete table, let me quickly refresh your mind on how to Insert table in Word 365.

As earlier said, when you open blank document, go straight to the **Insert** tab, and then click **Table** tool. Take your cursor down the boxes officially known as cells, and then click at a spot on the cells to insert a table.

Now, let me quickly walk you through on how to delete the inserted table in Microsoft Word 365. To delete table, take these steps:

- Drag your cursor to the start point of the table which shows symbol as **cross enclosed inside a box**

Fig 4.7: Drag your cursor to that point shown by the arrow

- Right-click your cursor at that point

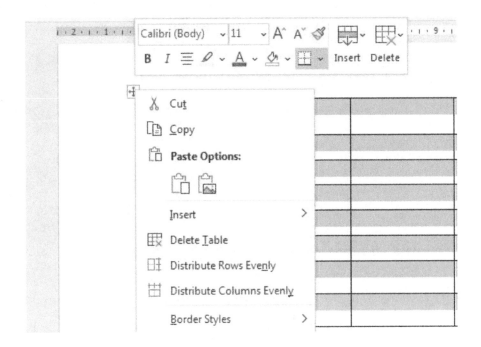

Fig 4.8: Options that will show up when you right-click at that point

- Select **Delete Table**

Once you click **Delete Table** option, the table you initially inserted in your Word 365 document will be deleted.

Completing Tasks Through Illustrations Category under Insert Tab

Illustrations is one of the categories of **Insert** tab. Through this section, you can complete many tasks in Word 365 effectively. In this subheading, I will take you on several step by step approaches to do certain thing in Microsoft Word 365.

Remember, to get to Illustrations in Word 365, you are to click your Word 365 for it to open and then select **Blank document** for the app to open fully. When you are on the Word environment, click **Insert** tab, and one of the categories that makes up the tab is labelled **Illustrations**.

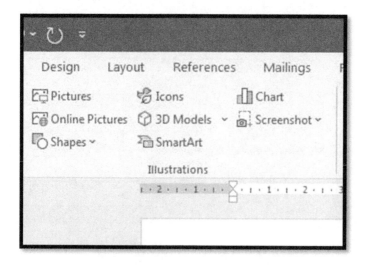

Fig 4.9: Screenshot of the Illustrations tool of Word 365

The lists available in **Illustrations** category are as follow:

- Pictures
- Online Pictures
- Shapes
- Icons
- 3D Models
- SmartArt
- Chart and
- Screenshot

Pictures

With the picture tools under the category named **Illustrations**, you can easily upload/Insert images in Word 365 document.

How to Insert Picture in Word 365
To insert image in Word 365, take the following steps:

- Click the Word 365 desktop application in your computer and select to open **Blank document**
- At the top part of the Word environment, click **Insert** tab
- Click **Pictures** button

Once you click **Pictures**, Word opens a folder in your computer. Select the right folder or place where the picture is in your computer.

- Double-click on the picture for it to be inserted in your document.

These are just simple steps to take to insert pictures in your newest version of Microsoft Word.

Online Pictures

With Online Pictures button, you can successfully insert pictures in Word directly from internet. This is another beauty that Microsoft team of technologists added into Word 365. So, if you are writing an academic project work for instance, you can obtain any picture you want to place in Word document directly from internet by clicking the **Online Pictures** button. When you click this button, a search box will be made available for you to search the image of the object you want in your document file.

How to obtain Picture Online Through Word 365 and Insert in the Document File Directly

These are the steps to achieve this task:

- Click the Word 365 desktop application in your computer and select to open **Blank document**
- At the top part of the Word environment, click **Insert** tab
- Click **Online Pictures** button
- Choose to search pictures through **Bing** or from **OneDrive**
- Type the name of the picture you want to insert

If for example I want to insert rose flower in the Word document, I will type rose flower in the search box and then search

- Click on any of the pictures you like and click **Insert** button which is below the search interface

Once you take the last step, the picture will be inserted inside your document.

Shapes

There are many shapes you can create using the **Shapes** tool of Word 365. I hope you have not forgotten how we got to this tool of Word 365. Let me quickly remind you should in case you have. To get to **Shapes** tool, click **Insert** and find **Shapes** in **Illustrations** category. When you click **Shapes**, it will open a new window showing you many shapes. You can select any shape of your choice and it will be inserted into your Word environment. From there, you can adjust it to the way you like to have it in Word.

Icons

Microsoft developed her Word 365 desktop application with many beautiful icons. You can find different kinds of icons in the icon tool.

How to Insert Icon in Word 365 Document

When you have already opened Blank document, to insert icon, take these steps:

- Click the **Insert** tab on top part of your document environment
- Click **Icons** button
- Select any icon you want to insert in the document
- Click **Insert** which appears at the bottom part of the icon gallery. You can drag the icon to any part of your document you want it to be.

3D Models Tool

With **3D Models** tool situated in **Insert** tab of Word 365, you can do some unique things. Word 365 supports inserting 3D models directly into documents. When the image is inserted, you can use the feature to illustrate a point. With this property, users can rotate models 360 degrees or tilt up and down to show a specific feature of an object. I will illustrate this practically to you for you to have deeper understanding of my explanation.

Working with 3D Models Tool in Word 365

To work with 3D Models tool, take the following steps:

- Click the **Insert** tab of Word 365 document

- Click **3D Models** which is one of the options available under the **Insert**

- As a new window opens when you click on the **3D Models,** you will be shown some pictures. The pictures are grouped into categories. If for example you click **Furniture**, you will be shown some pictures inside the Furniture category.

Fig 4.1.1: The 3D Models picture gallery that will show up when you click **3D Models**

- Insert any picture from the picture gallery in your Word environment by double-clicking on it

- At this state, you can press and hold the left part of your mouse and rotate the picture. That is the 3D model feature.

SmartArt

The **SmartArt** tool under **Insert** tab is used to communicate information virtually. It has graphical application. Through **SmartArt**, you will have access to many graphics integrated into Word 365 by Microsoft. SmartArt consists of many categories. The categories are **All, List, Process, Cycle, Hierarchy, Relationship, Matrix, Pyramid, Picture** and **Office.com**. Each of these categories contains graphics related to it. But **All** contains graphic designs that cut across the other categories.

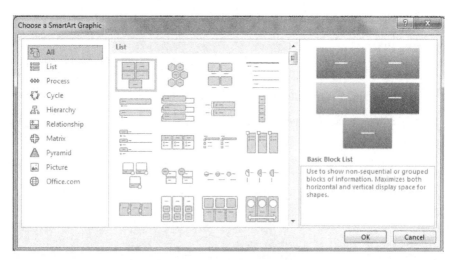

Fig 4.1.2: Picture showing the categories in SmartArt

In this section, I will walk you through on how to use SmartArt tool.

Step by Step Guide on how to use SmartArt Tool

To apply SmartArt tool in Word 365, take the following steps:

- Click your Word 365 to open and then select **Blank document** to open the Word environment

- Click **Insert** tab and select **SmartArt** which is in **Illustrations** category
- Select any graphic representation from the graphics category

You can choose from any category depending on what you are preparing. Take for instance I want to have graphical representation of salespersons positions in the company I work, I will choose one illustration under **Pyramid** category.

- Click **Ok** button

Once you click the **Ok** button at the right-hand side of the graphics gallery, the graphics will be inserted into your Word 365 environment.

- Start designing your graphics to fit into what you want to build at the end.

Since in this illustration I am building with pyramid to show the ranks of salespersons in insurance, I have to start my design. There is provision where I am to type texts and they reflect in the main pyramid stage. If I want to add more pyramid steps, I will right-click in any of the stage and select to **Add shape** option. From there I can choose to add the shape before or after. You can also adjust the position of the design by press and drag with your cursor.

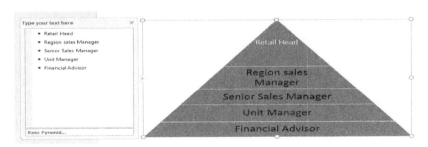

Fig 4.1.3: Picture shows the pyramid graphics design in progress obtained through **SmartArt** tool

- Click out of the section after design

Chart Tool in Illustrations Category

Chart is known to be important tool in the study of Mathematics and Statistics. With charts, you can illustrate different objects. Microsoft in her wisdom understand the importance of chart not only in schools but also in our daily activiies, and because of that integrate it in their word processing product. If you find yourself in certain enterprise, you will find out they make use of charts during presentations. The charts available in Word 365 are bar, area and line charts.

How to Create Chart in Word 365 Document

I assume that you have already opened blank document of Word 365 at this stage. To insert chart, take these steps:

- Click **Insert** tab at the top part of the Word environment
- Click **Chart** which is one of the buttons in **Illustrations** category
- Select the kind of the chart you want to build, and then click on any which fits into your plan properly

In this teaching, I want to build my presentation using column chart, so I have to click **Column**, and select **clustered column**.

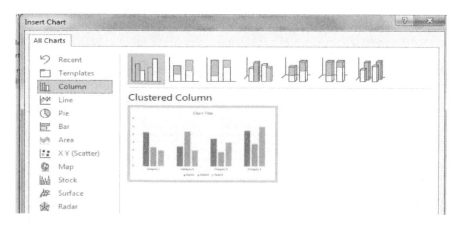

Fig 4.1.4: Building a clustered column chart in Word 365

- Click **Ok** button

When you click **Ok**, the chart is inserted in the document and you will see a picture like the one below:

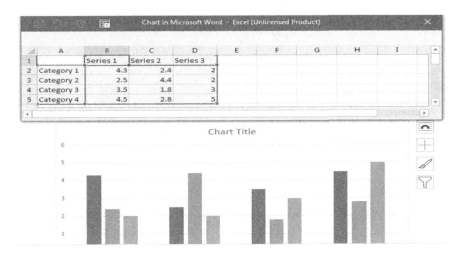

Fig 4.1.5: The chart template and chart editor section as inserted into Word 365

- Start designing your chart

You are to change the default data that is inserted in the chart. You are to change the side of the Excel document named **series** and **categories** to suit your own interest. Also, if you want to reduce the number of bars to two, all you have to do is to delete all the data in **column D**. On the other hand, if you want to increase the number of bars, create more columns with data. You can add more rows as well. Know that rows run horizontally while column runs vertically. The interesting thing about working on charts in Word 365 is that as you make changes, the changes reflects immediately in the bar.

Take for instance I want to show the percentage of consumption of three kinds of food in California from January to April. All I am to do is to change the default data that comes with my chart to my own data. At the end, I had my chart as below after preparing it.

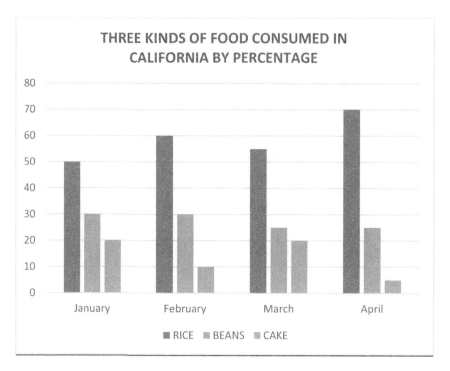

Fig 4.1.6: Prepared chart of three kinds of food and the percentage consumption

Note: if you want to change the data of your chart, you can right-click in the chart area and select **Edit Data** option.

Screenshot

The **Screenshot** feature in Word 365 is an added property by Microsoft company to her Word processing application. When I saw this new property in Word 365, I was glad it makes possible for users to easily take the screenshot of the Word environment when they work on it.

How to Take Screenshot in Word 365

To take screenshot in Word 365, take this my guide:

- Click your Word 365 app to open and choose to open **Blank document** or from Template
- Click **Insert** tab at the top part of the Word environment
- Select **Screenshot** button in **Illustrations** category

Once you click the **Screenshot** button, the Screenshot of the Word environment is taken immediately.

Chapter 5

How to make use of Other Tools in Insert Tab of Word 365

Word 365 is a great computer application, and because of that has a lot to write on it. In this chapter, I will continue from where I stop in the previous chapter. So, the learning is on how to complete other possible tasks which are possible through any tool available in **Insert** button of Word 365. Without taking much time in this introduction, let us get started.

The Components of Add-ins Category

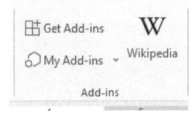

Fig 5: The **Add-ins** Category under **Insert** menu shown

As shown in the picture above, the components of **Add-ins** category are **Get Add-ins**, **My Add-ins** and **Wikipedia**. As the component names sound, so is their roles. I will explain further.

Working with Add-ins Category
Just like any other tool used in Word 365, **Add-ins** tool is one of them. The **Add-ins** can be found when you click **Insert** menu. When you enable **Add-**

ins in Word 365, it adds custom commands and new features to Office programs. This makes you to work more productively in the Word application. With Add-ins security settings feature, you can deny hackers access to your important Word files. Add-ins can be purchased from its developers online and they get installed in your Word 365. But before you install any add-ins in your Word 365, make sure you trust the source.

Get Add-ins

When you click **Get Add-ins,** a new window opens in Word showing some add-ins which you can purchase or get for free from the Office store. The screenshot is shown below:

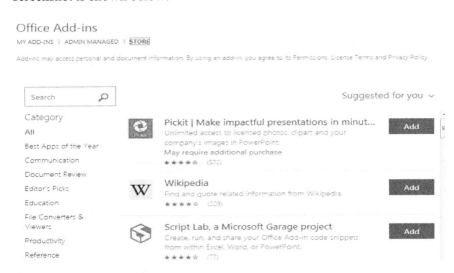

Fig 5.1: Store to buy and install add-ins in Word 365

Make sure your computer is connected to internet before you click **Get Add-ins.** If you have any add-in in mind before clicking the **Get Add-ins** button, you can search for it using the search box on the top part of the interface. Click **Add** button, grant permission to install the add-in in your Word 365, and then start making use of it after the installation.

My Add-ins

Through **My Add-ins** button, you can see the add-ins you have already installed in your Word 365. By default, if you click that button, it will give you the notification that you have no add-ins installed in your Word app. But if you have installed any in your Word app and click on it, it will show you the available one. You can also delete already installed add-in which you do not want to have again through this tool.

Wikipedia

Microsoft which is the developer of Word 365 has good relationship with Wikipedia. As a result of that, they have inactive Wikipedia add-in in the **Add-ins** category under **Insert** in Word 365. This makes it easy for you to enable it in your Word. When you click the **Wikipedia** add-in, the system will ask you for permission to install the add-in in your Word 365 as shown below:

Fig 5.2: Permission request to enable Wikipedia add-in in Word 365

So, from the picture, once you give permission by clicking the **Trust this add-in** button, the Wikipedia add-in will be installed in your Word app.

Media Category

Media is one of the categories in **Insert** menu of Word 365 computer application. What it implies is that when you open **Blank document** or document **template** of Word 365 and click the **Insert** menu, one of the sub sections inside that **Insert** menu is **Media**.

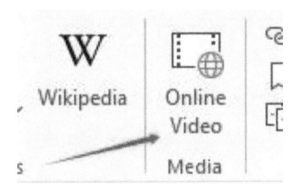

Fig 5.3: Media section of Word 365 shown by the arrow

Through the Media, you can insert videos obtained from the internet into your Word 365 document.

Step by Step Guide on how to Insert Videos Available on Internet into Word 365 Document

To successfully complete this task, make sure your computer is connected to internet. To achieve the main task, take these steps:

- Open Word 365 document in your computer by clicking the app and then select to open **Blank document** or any **template** document
- Click **Insert** tab at the top of the Word environment
- Click **Online Video** button which I grouped into Media Category

As you click **Online Video**, a new box opens requesting you inside the URL or embed code of the online video. Please know that URL is the address of a web page. And in this discussion, it means the link where the video can be found online. Example of an online video URL in youtube.com is https://m.youtube.com/watch?v=YWA-xbsJrVg

- Copy the video URL or embed code from the online source
- Paste the link in the dialog box

Fig 5.4: Paste it in the box as shown above

- Click **Insert** button of the dialog box

As you click on **Insert** button at the bottom of the box, the video will gradually be inserted into your Word 365 document. Once the video is inserted in your word file, you can click on the play button and the video starts playing inside the Word document without going to the website where the video link is located. This is a welcomed development from Microsoft Corporation.

Links Category in Insert Menu

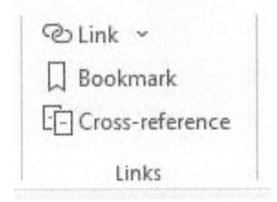

Fig 5.5: The components of the **Links** category in **Insert** tab

As the name implies, you can place links in Word 365 data using the tools available in this section. The components of the Links category are Hyperlink, Bookmark, and Cross-Reference.

Link

You can create a link in your document for quick access to webpages and other files using the **Hyperlink** button. A hyperlink is defined as a link from a hypertext document to another location, activated by clicking on a highlighted word or image. When you highlight any picture or texts you want to hyperlink and click the **Hyperlink** button, "**Insert Hyperlink**" dialog box shows up. You can then insert your link inside the box and click **Ok**. Whenever a reader of the document clicks on the hyperlinked text or picture, the person is directed to the webpage where he or she can read further.

Bookmark

The Bookmark tool in **Insert** displays the "Bookmark" dialog box when clicked. You can save some important links using this tool.

Cross-Reference

When **Cross-Reference** tool is clicked, it displays the "Cross Reference" dialog box. This tool allows users cross reference other parts of their document. It is used for figure numbers and section headings.

How to Hyperlink Texts and Pictures in Word 365

In this teaching, I assume that you have already opened Blank document. So, to insert links or pictures in Word 365 take these steps:

- Highlight the texts or picture you want to hyperlink
- Copy the link from the web where it is located but if you want to link between document file in your computer, you do not need to copy any web link

If for example you want to insert the web address *www.amazon.com* in texts in your document, then copy it from the web or ignore if you can easily enter it when the time comes without making mistake.

- Click the **Insert** tab
- Locate **Link** button by the top right-hand side, which is in **Links** category, and click it. You will see a dialog box appear on your computer screen when you click **Link** as shown below:

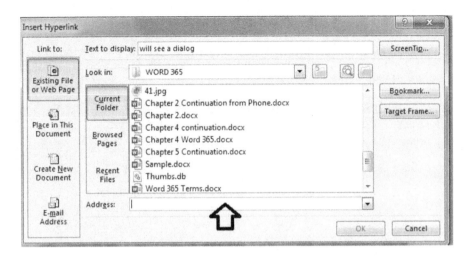

Fig 5.6: Dialog box to insert weblink or link any document in your computer

If it is a weblink you want to link, then type the weblink in the **Address** as shown by the arrow. If I want to link to Amazon website for instance, I will paste www.amazoncom in the **Address** box. But if I want to link the document in my computer, I will locate the document file and select it.

- Click **Ok** button, and the hyperlink is established

Note: Before now, if you hyperlink texts or pictures in the older versions of Microsoft Words, simple click on the hyperlinked texts or picture will take you to the original location of the link. But for you to be taken to the location of the link or document in Word 365, you are to use the shortcut **Ctrl + Click**. Please take note of this change.

How to Insert Bookmark in Word 365 Document

To bookmark any part of your Word document, example the chapters and subheadings, take the following steps:

- As the Word document is opened, select/highlight the titles and subheadings you want to bookmark

- Click **Insert** tab
- Click **Bookmark** tool which is in **Links** category for a dialog box to display as shown below:

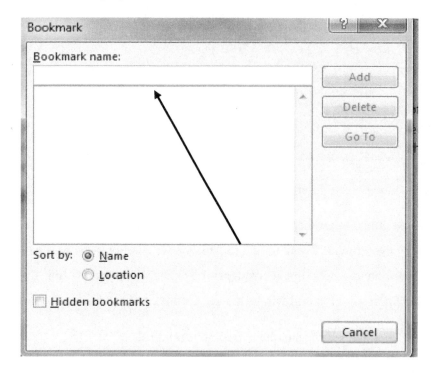

Fig 5.7: Dialog box to set up bookmark information

- Write the name you want to give the bookmarked heading or subheading in the **Bookmark name** section

Please do not space the words that makes the title. If you do that, the **Add** button by the right will not be enabled.

- Click **Add** button for the bookmark to be added

How to Access and Delete your Bookmarks in Word 365
If you want to access or delete your bookmarks, take these steps:

- As you document is opened, click the **Insert** tab

72

- Select **Bookmark** tool in Links category

As you click the **Bookmark** tool, a dialog box shows up which displays the bookmarks you have added in your Word.

- To access any of the bookmarks, click on it and click the **Go To** button. This action will take you directly to the section of that document.
- If you want to delete the bookmark, just select it and then click **Delete** button.

Step by Step Guide on how to Cross-reference in Word 365

In this section, I will teach you how to cross-reference between table of contents of a book and the book chapters that are in the book body section. From this teaching, you will learn how to cross-reference to other parts of a document, example subheadings of a book if you want to do so in your linking task.

Know that before you cross-reference to different parts of a document, example chapters section, you are to make the title and subtitle texts headings. So, I will teach you how to create headings in Word document first before going into cross-reference. If you can remember, I have taught this before under **Home** tab but let me repeat it.

Headings Creation in Word

I assume that you have written your book or article chapters in your Word document accordingly and want to make them your headings. To create headings, take the following steps:

- Select the chapter text of your book, example chapter 1
- Click the **Home** tab of your Word 365

- Click **Heading 1** or **Heading 2** under Styles category

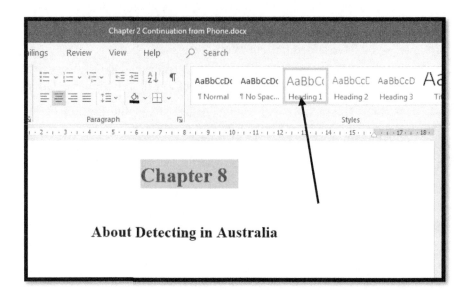

Fig 5.8: The Heading under **Home** tab shown

Once you select any of the Headings, the text color of the text you are styling will change (mainly blue color). You can make the text bold by using the bold tool, align it to the center or justify, or even change the font and the font size.

Follow this step to create as many headings you want for cross-reference as possible. If for instance the book is made of 8 chapters and you want to cross-reference 8 of them, create 8 headings. Each time you create a new heading, it is added to the cross-link section but that is not shown to you until you start the cross-referencing.

Know that in this sample I want a situation whereby when readers click the chapter in my table of contents, they will be taken to the main chapter in the body of the eBook.

Back to Cross-Reference

Since we have created headings, to cross-reference, take these steps:

- Highlight the texts which you want to link from

Since I am cross-linking from the chapter of the book from the table of contents, I will highlight the chapter I have at the table of contents section of the book.

- Click the **Insert** tab at the top left-hand corner of the tab section of Word 365

- Select **Cross-reference** tool which is in **Links** category which will display the dialog box like the one below:

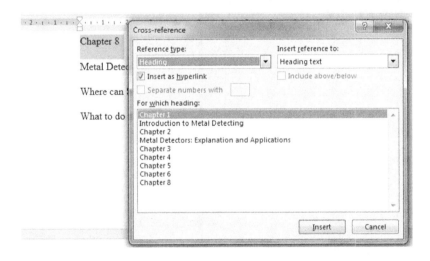

Fig 5.9: The screenshot of the dialog box that will display when **Cross-reference is clicked**

In the **Reference type**, choose **Heading**, and in **Insert reference** to, choose **Heading text**. Check the box at **Insert as hyperlink**. From the screenshot, I was trying to cross-reference **chapter 8**, so, at **For Which heading**, I would select **Chapter 8**.

- Click **Insert** which is at the button.

So, repeat this process for all the chapters of your book you want to cross-link. At the end, if a reader uses the command **Ctrl + Click** on the chapter section of the table of content, he or she will be taken to the body section of the individual chapters of the book.

Comments Category in Insert
This is another important arear in the **Insert** tab of Word 365. With Comment tool, you can make suggestions to other people or track issues for follow-up.

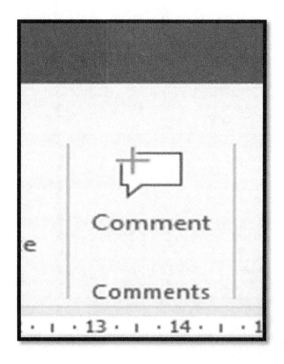

Fig 5.1.1: The **Comment** tool in **Insert** tab

Let as assume that you are a teacher that teach students in a secondary school, you can use the comment tool to pass extra information to your students. Also, if for instance someone sent a statement of account using

Word 365 document, you highlight the part of the statement of account you do not understand and comment before sending back to the sender. You can write in the statement that you do not understand the Mathematics in a particular area of the account statement. When he or she reads the comment, the replies to the comment and sends back to you.

How to Insert a Comment
To insert a comment in texts, take these steps:

- Highlight the texts you want to insert comments in
- Click the **Insert** tab at the top part of your Word 365 document
- Click the **Comment** tool under the Comments category
- Type your comment. When you type your comment, Word shows your comment in a balloon in the document's margin.
- When you are done typing, just click into Word document environment to exit the comment section. That is all.

When you send the document out, the reader will see the comment by the margin and then reply if necessary.

The Header & Footer Category in Insert Tab
This is a basic section in Word 365. The **Header & Footer** category is made up of **Header**, **Footer** and **Page Number**.

A **Header** is the top margin of each page of Word document, and a **Footer** is the bottom margin of each page. Have you picked a book and as you were reading the book saw the title of the book written at the top margin of the pages? The title written on the top part was made possible with the help of **Header** tool. Also, page numbers of books are written on the **Footer** section of Word document.

How to insert Text at the Header Section of Word 365 Document
Follow this guide to insert text at the Header section of your word document:

- Open your Word 365 document

- Select the **Insert** tab of the Word 365 document

- Click **Header** button which is in the **Header & Footer** category

- Choose the build-in header of your choice preferably the first on the list

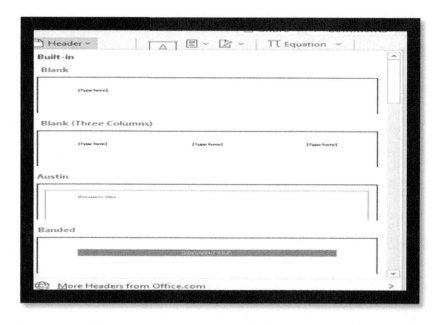

Fig 5.1.2: Click on any of the build-in header type

Fig 5.1.3: Type in your text in the section shown

- Type in your text

If I want to use the title of this my book on the header section for instance, I will type "WORD FOR MICROSOFT 365 FOR BEGINNERS" in that section. You can change the font size of the text by highlighting the text and then choose the **Font Size** tool in **Home** tab.

- Double-click at the body part of your Word to exit the header section

How to Access Footer Section
To access the footer of Word 365 document, take the following steps:

- Open your Word 365 document
- Select the **Insert** tab of the Word 365 document
- Click **Footer** button which is in the **Header & Footer** category
- Select the footer style you want from the options that will be displayed

Once you take the above last, the Footer section of the document will be opened.

- You can then insert texts or page numbers at the footer
- Once you are through with the texts or number you want to insert at the footer, double-click at any body part of your Word document or just click the **Close Header and Footer** button at the top right-hand side of toolbar section of Word 365.

Fig 5.1.4: **Close Header and Footer** shown by the arrow

Page Number

The **Page Number** tool in Header & Footer category is used to number the pages of Word documents. With this tool, you can choose how you want to number the pages of you document. Page Number is one of the major tools used by book writers frequently during formatting of their books. I will teach you how to number pages in Word 365, and how to number parts of a Word document differently.

How to Number Document Pages

To number document pages in Word 365, take these steps

- As you are done with typing in Word 365 document, click **Insert** tab

- Click **Page Number** button which is in the **Header and Footer** category

This will show some options. The options are possible areas where you want to insert your page numbers.

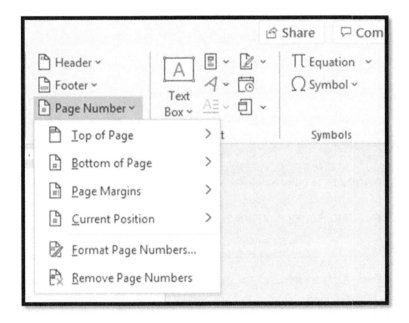

Fig 5.1.5: Options to choose where you want to insert your page numbers

- The common section of document where users insert page number is at the bottom of the pages, so you can click **Bottom of Page** option
- Select any of the **Bottom of Page** samples

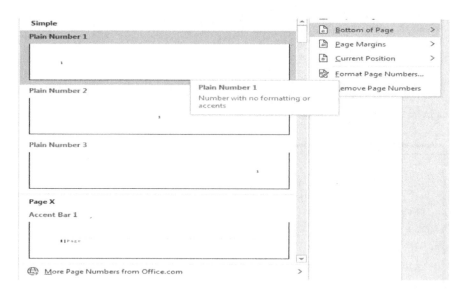

Fig 5.1.6: Bottom of the page samples

As you select a sample, page numbers are automatically inserted on your document pages.

How to Add Different Page Numbers Formats to Different Sections in Word 365

Numbering pages differently in Words was one of the major formatting issues I had when I started publishing books newly. When I finished writing my book and remembered page numbering for the paper format, I usually got tired. In this section, I will help you solve the challenge.

Take for instance you finished writing a book and you do not want to have any page number on the copyright page, want to number the acknowledgement and the table of content pages with i, ii, iii… format, and number from the chapter 1 page to the end with 1, 2, 3… numbering format, then how do you go about it?

In that case, you are to break different parts of the pages into sections. After that, you are to unlink these sections from each other. The next is choosing different page numbering formats for the individual document sections.

Let us get started

Take these practical steps to number sections of your Word 365 document differently:

- Click your computer cursor at the end of the last line on the page where you want to start your page section break

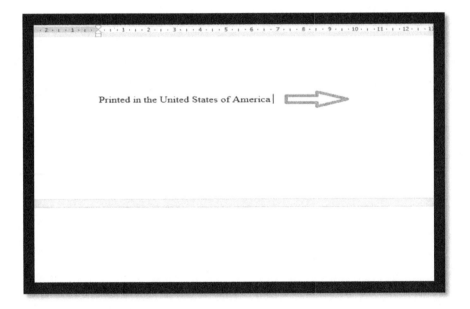

Fig 5.1.7: The last line of the page where I want to start creating my page section

In this teaching, my first page is the Copyright section so I will click my cursor on that page.

- Click the **Layout** tab

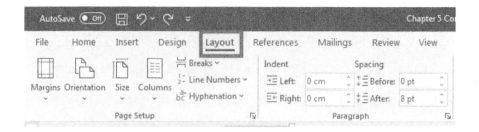

Fig 5.1.8: **Layout** tab indicated in the picture

- Click **Breaks** and select **Next Page** under **Section Breaks**

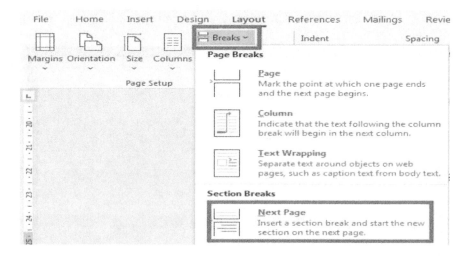

Fig 5.1.9: Click **Breaks** and select **Next Page**

When you click **Next Page**, the texts on the next page may be moved forward, just use your keyboard's backspace key to bring them back to their initial position on the page.

- Take your computer cursor to the end of the last line on the page where you want to start another page section

Here, I want to create another page section which will separate my table of content from the main book section. Remember, I want to have separate section of Copyright page, separate table of contents section, and separate main book section which will show the main contents of my book from chapter one to the end. So, in respect to this explanation, I take my cursor to the end of the last line of my books table of contents and click after the last text.

Chapter 8

Metal Detecting in Germany

Where can Someone find Gold in Germany?

What you need when you find yourself in Germany for Metal Hunt

Fig: 5.2.1: My cursor placed after the last text of the table of contents section of my book

- Click the **Layout** tab
- Click **Breaks** and select **Next Page** under **Section Breaks**

This last action will create another page section in your word document. In these total narration in creating of page sections, I ended up having three sections of the document. I have the Copyright, table of contents section, and the Main book section. To see all the section breaks you have in your document, click your Word's **Home** tab and then **Show/Hide Paragraph** tool represented as inverted **P** as shown below:

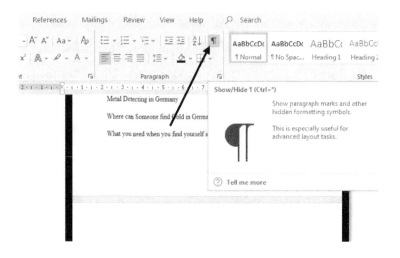

Fig 5.2.2: The **Show/Hide Paragraph** tool

To exit the Show/Hide tool, still click the tool.

Let us start the page numbering of the different sections

To number the different page sections with different number formats, take these steps

- Click the **Insert** tab
- Click **Page Number**, Select **Bottom of Page** option and then choose any style sample

Immediate you take above action; the same page numbers format will be assigned to all the pages of the document. Do not worry because it will be fixed.

- Scroll up to first page of your first section break
- Click the footer section where the page number is inserted

Fig 5.2.3: The footer of the Section 1 of my document

The above page is the Copyright section of my book and I do not want to number it, as a result of that, I have to delete that page number "**1**". But if in your own document you want to start your numbering from i, ii, iii…. That I will teach you in the next step.

- Scroll down to the footer of the first page of the next section (that is section 2 using my teaching sample) and then number the pages of the document using different page number format.

Fig 5.2.4: The section 2 of my document, which is the table of contents of my book.

- Uncheck the box **Different First Page** and that of **Different Odd & Even Pages**. Only leave the box **Show Document Text** checked as shown in the picture above.

- Click **Link to Previous** to deselect the link between the previous section 1 from the current section. When you do this, it reminds the system to number the present section differently.

- Click the **Page Number** which now appears at the top right-hand side as shown in the above picture and select **Format Page Numbers....** which is explain through this picture below:

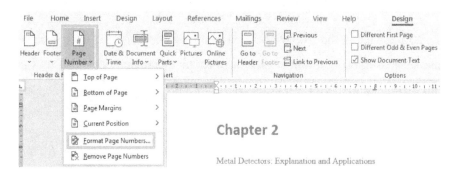

Fig 5.2.5: Page number formatting in Progress

As you click the **Format Page Numbers....**, the dialog box below will be shown to you:

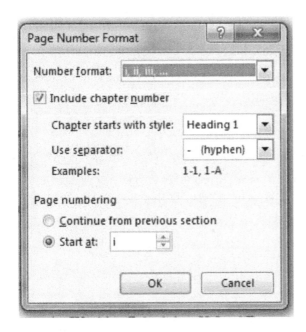

Fig 5.2.6: Choosing the page number format and settings

From the above dialog box, you are to choose the page numbering format you want in that page section and other settings relating to it. In my own case, since I am formatting the table content which is in the Section 2 I created, in the **Number format**, I am choosing **i, ii, iii, ...** but you can choose any page number format depending on the area of the book you are working on. Uncheck Include chapter number if that page section does not contain chapters. Since I am on the table of contents section of my book, I will uncheck it because it does not have chapters as I have in the main book content. Enable **Start at** by just clicking on it. By default, it selects "**i**" but you can insert which number you want it to start from if not fine by you.

- Click **ok** button for your command to be established.
- When you clicked **Ok** in the above step, the page number will not be inserted on the page as programmed but you need to take little more steps to make it work

- Click **Page Number**, and then select **Bottom of Page**, followed by any page number sample. Immediately you take this action, the page numbers will be inserted in those pages of that section in the format you want them.

Fig: 5.2.7: Part of the above explanation in picture

Now, numbering the book main pages in numbers (Section 3)

Numbering the page numbers of the major book content which I have in the section 3 of this teaching involves same steps. What you are to do is just to choose the numbering format as 1, 2, 3…. when the format dialog box displays. Other steps remain same. But let me make it more detailed.

- Scroll down to the footer of the first page of the next section (that is section 3 using my teaching sample) and then number the pages of the document using different page number format.
- Uncheck the box **Different First Page** and that of **Different Odd & Even Pages**. Only leave the box **Show Document Text** checked as shown in the picture where I explained section 2 pages numbering.
- Click **Link to Previous** to deselect the link between the previous section 2 from the current section 3. When you do this, it reminds the system to number the present section 3 differently.

- Click the **Page Number** which now appears at the top right-hand side and select **Format Page Numbers....**

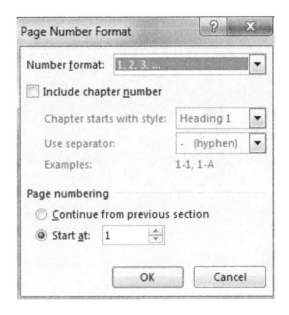

Fig 5.2.8: Page number format for the book main content

From the above dialog box, you are to choose the page numbering format you want in that page section and other settings relating to it. In my own case, since I am formatting the main book content which is in the Section 3 I created, in the **Number format**, I am choosing **1, 2, 3, ...** but you can choose any page number format depending on the area of the book you are working on. Uncheck **Include chapter number**. Enable **Start at** by just clicking on it. By default, it selects "**1**" which is fine for me, but you can insert which number you want it to start from if not fine by you.

- Click **ok** button for your command to be established.
- When you clicked **Ok** in the above step, the page number will not be inserted on the page as programmed but you need to take little more steps to make it work.

- Click **Page Number**, and then select **Bottom of Page**, followed by any page number sample. Immediately you take this action, the page numbers will be inserted in those pages of that section 3 in the format you want them.

The Text Category in Insert Tab

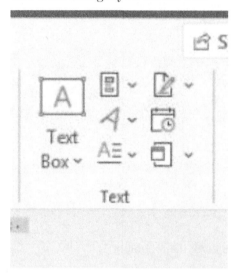

Fig 5.2.9: The **Text** category in **Insert** tab

Text is a category in the **Insert** menu of Word 365 document. The tools in this part of **Insert** are **Text Box, Explore Quick Parts, WordArt, Drop Cap, Signature Line**, **Date and Time**, and **Object**. You can use the components available in this section of **Insert** to shape and style texts. One of the major components in **Text** is **Text Box**.

How to Insert Text Box in Word
The steps to insert text box in Word are as follow:

- Open **Blank document** of your Word 365
- Click the **Insert** tab
- Click the **Text Box** tool in **Text** category of **Insert**

As you click the **Text Box** tool, the cursor pointer changes into a crosshair symbol.

- Take the cursor pointer to the part of the Word document where you want to draw the text box
- Press and drag your mouse to draw your text box
- Remove your finger from the cursor to release the pressure
- Click inside the text box and start typing your texts inside

These are just the steps to follow to create text box and insert texts inside it as well.

With **Explore Quick Parts**, you can insert preformatted texts, auto-text, document properties and fields in Word 365 document. **WordArt** tool on the other hand allows users of Word 365 to add artistic flair to their texts. I have explained this in one of the previous chapters.

Drop Cap tool is used to add big capital letter at the beginning of a paragraph. It is usually used to start letters in book or article chapters. To insert drop cap at any paragraph, take these steps:

- Take your cursor to where you want to insert drop cap and select the first letter of the word
- Click **Insert** tab
- Select **Drop Cap** tool in **Text** category
- From the options that will be displayed, click **Dropped**.

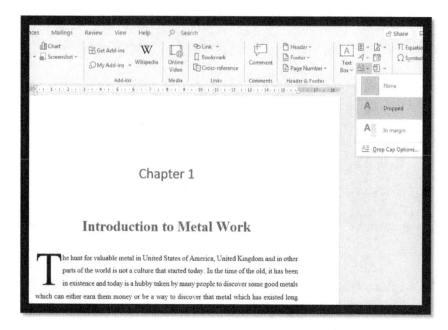

Fig 5.3.1: Placing Drop Cap in Word document paragraph

Signature Line in **Text category** of **Insert** tab is used to add signature to your already typed document. With this tool, Word 365 users can add a signature line to a document or add a graphic of their handwritten signature. Also, you can save a signature block as an AutoText building block using this tool.

Date and Time tool is used to add date and time in Word 365 document. The **Object** on the other hand allows you to insert embedded objects in Word 365 document. Examples of embedded objects are Excel chart or another word document.

The Symbols Category of Insert Tab

Mathematics equations and symbols are important in our lives today. I know that you as a reader of this book has solved Mathematics in one time or the other of your life. That is to tell you it is important. Because of its importance, Microsoft saw it as something vital to integrate into their Word processing application. The last category of **Insert** tab is named **Symbols**. This category contains varieties of symbols and Equations. Through it, you can insert symbols and equations in Word 365 document.

Chapter 6

Design and Customization in Word 365

This is a new chapter where you will learn important skills on the **Design** tab and customization in Word 365. I will make sure I do justice to this area of study in Word 365. There are some hidden skills in these areas you do not know.

Word 365 computer applications comes with many designs. These designs were integrated into the application to leave us who are the users with many choices. In that case, there are many designs for different kinds of document.

Thorough **Design** tab, of Word 365 application, you can choose any document new style set for your document. In fact, you can create a new document theme for yourself through this tool and use it for any other document you want to build in Word application. Many letter headings you see used by many companies were designed thorough this tab.

There are some companies that have the picture or logo of their companies at the background of their letter headings. Such task can be completed using the Watermarks tool in **Design** of Word applications. Do not worry because I will walk you through on how to do that on your own without much stress.

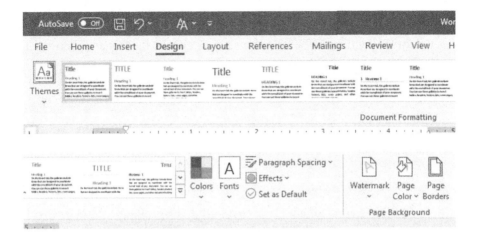

Fig 6: Screenshot showing Design tab of Word 365 and the components

The Tools in Design Tab

The tools available in **Design** tab of Word 365 are:

- Theme
- Document formatting
- Color
- Fonts
- Paragraph Spacing
- Effects
- Set as Default
- Page Background

Theme is the first tool in Design tab of Word 365. When a theme is applied in document, it changes an entire document and gives it a different and professional look. When you click **Theme**, you will be shown many themes available in Word 365. Some of the names of themes in Word 365 are Office, Gallery, Facet, Integral, Ion, Ion Board, Organic, Retrospect, Slice, Wisp, Banded, Basis, Berlin, Circuit, Damask, Dividend, Droplet, Frame and Main Event. When you set your word document title using the **Heading** tool under

Home tab and then apply any of these themes, you will see how your document look will be. You can also save any of the themes and then use it to create presentation file in Microsoft PowerPoint application. The themes in Word 365 app are great and dynamic.

How to Choose and Apply Document Theme
To choose and apply document theme in Word 365, take these steps:

- Click **Design** tab
- Click **Theme**, which is the first tool in the group
- Click any of the available themes displayed to you and it will be applied

How to Change Theme Color
Without taking much of your time, to change the color of the theme to be applied in your document, take these steps:

- Click **Design** tab
- Select **Colors** tool
- Point to a color to preview how it will look in your document.
- Click a color scheme.

Document formatting in Design Tab Explained
When choose any **Theme** design through the **Design** tab of your Word 365, the document formatting section shows you different ways you can change your document design further. Each of those designs is designed starting with the heading **Title**. After you have taken the necessary steps to make the document look as shown in the interface and click on any of the document formatting designs, your document will change to the design you select.

Fig 6.1: Document formatting section indicated

Color Tool in Design Tab

With **Color** tool, you can choose the color of your document title as well as the color of the texts of the document design you choose. You may like to have the heading to be in green color and the texts that make up the rest of the document in black. This can be achieved using the **Color** tool.

Fonts in Design Tab

With **Fonts**, you can choose from the many available fonts integrated into Word 365 **Design** tab by the Microsoft application developers. There are many captivating fonts you can choose from just to fit into the document design you want to create. At the end, you will be happy with the document you have. When you click **Fonts**, you will see some of the fonts in the **Fonts** tool.

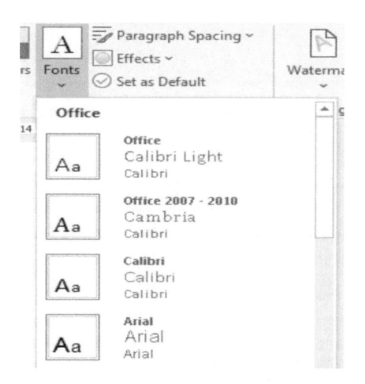

Fig 6.2: Some of the fonts available in the **Font** tool of **Design** tab

As seen above, when you click the **Fonts** button, you will be shown fonts you can choose from. As you scroll down, you will be shown more. And as your cursor gets to any of the fonts, you will be shown in the title texts how it will appear when select in as much as you have made the title a heading using the **Headings** tool at the **Home** tab first.

Paragraph Spacing tool in Design Tab
With the **Paragraph Spacing** tool, you can select any paragraph spacing you want to apply on the document you are designing. When you click the Paragraph Spacing button, you will be shown Paragraph menu and from there make your choice.

Effects Tool in Design Tab of Word 365 Explained

Effects tool allows you to add effects to your document. In a more detailed way, theme **Effects** include shadows, reflections, lines, fills, and more. You cannot create your own set of theme effects, but you can pick any set of effects that you feel will work well for the document you are creating. When you click **Effects**, you will be shown those that are available.

Set as Default

With this tool, you can use any document theme you have created as you default document style. In this case, anytime you open your Word 365 document theme section, that theme will be chosen as your default document design theme.

Page Background under Design Tab

The **Page Background** group/category of **Design** tab is made up of three major tools. These tools are **Watermark**, **Page Color** and **Page Borders**.

The term **Watermark** means a faint design made in document that is visible when looked closely at or held against the light depending on how faint the design is. **Watermark** can be created in Word 365 document using the Watermark tool in **Design** tab.

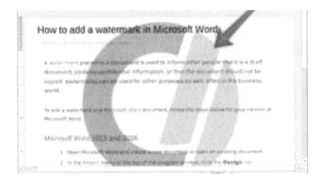

Fig 6.3: Example of Word document designed with Watermark

How to Insert Watermark in Document create with Word 365 Application

To complete this task, take the following steps:

- Click the **Design** tab

- Select **Watermark**

- Choose a pre-configured watermark, like DRAFT or CONFIDENTIAL or customize your own

Fig 6.4: Choosing a predesigned watermark or customize your own

To customize your own watermarks as shown in the picture (example your company's logo or picture), click **Custom Watermark**. When you choose that option, you will see the dialog box below:

Fig 6.5: Customization of Watermark for Word 365 document in progress

Choose **Picture Watermark if you** have any picture or logo in your computer you want to use as your watermark, and then click **Select Picture**. When you click the button, the system will ask you to choose from the place you want to get your picture and you are to select from the options. If your computer is not connected to the internet when you want to choose the picture, you will see a notification informing you that your computer is not connected to the internet. Click the **Work offline** button and upload the picture you want to use from your computer. Untick the **Washout** box so that your watermark will not be too faint.

You can also customize texts as your watermark. If you want to do so, check the **Text watermark** box. Insert the text you want to use as watermark in the space provided for you.

- Click **Apply** button for the watermark to be applied in your document
- Close the Watermark dialog box

Page Color and Page Borders in Design Tab

Page Color and **Page Borders** are among the three tools in **Page Background** group of **Design** tab. With Page color, you can choose the color you want the document page you build through **Design** tab to have. There are various of colors available. To change the page color, just click your cursor at any spot in the document, click the **Page Color** tool and then select a color of your choice. As you hover your cursor over any of the colors, you will see how the document color will be if you finally select it.

Page Borders tool allows you to set the border of any document you want to create thorough Design tab. Just click the **Page Borders** tool and a dialog box will open. Within the box, set the borders of the document you want to create and apply it.

How to Build Letter Heading Document Using Word 365 Through Design Tab

In this section, I will apply the teaching I have given to you so far in this chapter to create fresh letter heading. In this chapter, I assumed I have a construction company and hence wants to build a letter heading for it. To build a letter heading, the first step to take after typing your title is to convert the title texts to heading by highlighting the texts and then click any of the **Headings** tool at the **Home** tab to convert the texts originally to heading. Also know that for **Themes** under **Design** tab to work, you must first convert the title text to heading.

To create document letter heading, follow these step by step guide:

- Open your Blank document and type in your texts

These texts should include your letter heading title section, the address, email address and mobile phone number. Example is the one I created by myself which is shown below:

SMART CONSTRUCTION COMPANY

No 16 Bills Street	Email: contact@smartcompany.com	Phone: +1-541-754-2248
California		+1-541-754-8748
United State		+1-541-754-2276

Fig 6.6: Screenshot showing my texts for letter heading creation

In the above picture, **SMART CONSTRUCTION COMPANY** is the title of my document.

- Select the title texts of the document, click the **Home** tab of Word 365 and then click the **Heading 1** or **Heading 2** to change the title text to heading.
- You can align the Heading text to center after the above step, change the font and make it bolder
- Click the **Design** tab
- Click **Theme** and select any theme of your choice
- Click **Colors** tool and select themes color you want to have
- From the **Document formatting** group, you can select any document style that will be nice for your letter heading document
- Click **Font** tool which is in **Design** tab to select any font for your texts
- Click **Watermark**
- Select **Custom Watermark** with the assumption that you already have the picture or logo of the document you want to use as watermark
- When you choose that option, you will see the dialog box below:

Fig 6.7: Setting up custom watermark

- Check **Picture Watermark** button.
- Click **Select Picture**

When you click the button, the system will ask you to choose from the place you want to get you picture and you are to select from the options. If your computer is not connected to the internet when you want to choose the picture, you will see a notification informing you that your computer is not connected to the internet. Click the **Work offline** button and upload the picture you want to use from your computer.

- Untick the **Washout** box so that your watermark will not be too faint.
- Click **Apply** button for the watermark to be applied in your document

- Close the Watermark dialog box

Fig 6.8: The design I had after creating my letter heading

With this design, I can use the document as letter heading to print letters.

Customization of Ribbons in Word 365

In this last subheading of this chapter, I will walk you through on how to customize ribbons in your Word 365 application. The Ribbon is a user interface element which was introduced by Microsoft in Microsoft Word computer application and has made working with the application easy. By default, the ribbon of Word 365 shows ten tabs; File, Home, Insert, Design, Layout, References, Mailing, Review, View and Help. But, the total number of main tabs that are in Word 365 are more than that when you access the Customize Ribbon section through the **Word Options**.

You may decide to rearrange or remove any of your major tabs from Word interface but may not know how to go about it. In this section, I will guide you through.

How to Access Ribbon in Word 365

To access the Ribbon section of Word 365, take the following steps:

- Open the Blank document of your Word 365 application
- Click the **File** tab

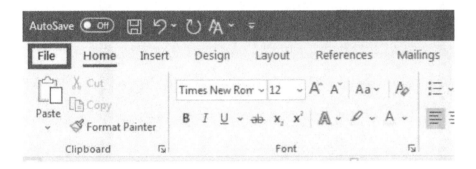

Fig 6.9: The **File** tab of Word 365 document indicated

- Click **Options** which is the last tool among others in the list
- In the dialog box that will show up, click **Customize Ribbon**

As you click the **Customize Ribbon** as I instructed above, you will be shown the major tabs on your Word document tab section.

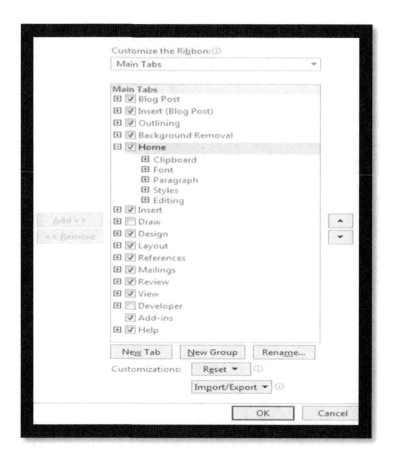

Fig 6.1.1: Main tabs on my Word shown through ribbon

From the picture shown above, you can choose to remove any tab from displaying at the Word tab section. You can also make a tab comes before the other (rearrangement of tabs). You can also give the tabs any name of your choice.

To remove any tab from the ribbon so it does not appear on the Word tab section, just uncheck the box showing the name of the Tab and click Ok

To rename a tab, just right click at the tab as shown in the picture and chose **Rename** *option. Type the new name you want the table to answer and apply it.*

To reorder any tab, just click the tab you want to move and the click the move up or move down arrow. Then click **OK** *button at the bottom for the change to be saved.*

Chapter 7

Understanding Document Layout of Word 365

A new page has been opened for a new class of teaching on Word 365 use and practice. The **Layout** tab of Word 365 is one of the frequently used tabs. In this chapter, I will guide you through on some important tasks you can complete through this tab.

Groups/Categories in Layout Tab

Fig 7: The Layout tab and the categories in picture

Whether I call it groups or categories, I am still referring to the same area of interest. The tools in the **Layout** tab of Word 365 is grouped. The categories in the tab are as follow:

- Page Setup
- Paragraph and
- Position

Page Setup Category of Layout Tab

With the tools in the **Page Setup** group you can set any document you are creating to the standard you want it. If you are new to Word 365 and want to locate the **Page Setup** group, just click on **Layout** tab, and there is it looking at you. The page setup are the parameters defined by the user that help determine how a printed page appears. The components of the page Setup category are **Margins, Orientation, Size, Columns, Breaks, Line Numbers,** and **Hyphenation.**

How to Setup Margins

With **Margins** tool, you can set up document margins in Word 365 application. In Word processing, a margin is the space between the text and the edge of your document. When you install your Word 365 application, the margins are set to **Normal**. What that implies is that it has a one-inch space between the text and each edge.

To setup margin in your Word document, take these steps:

- Open the **Blank document** of your Word 365
- Click **Layout** tab
- Click **Margins** which is under **Page Setup** category

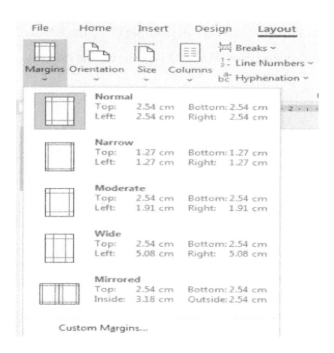

Fig 7.1: Screenshot of what are available when you click **Margins** tool

As seen in the above picture, just click on any margin you want your document to be in and your word document will take that margin. If you want a custom margin, just click **Custom Margins...** and then set it up in the dialog box that will be displayed to you. When you are done setting it up, just click **Ok** for your change to be saved.

How to Choose page Orientation in Word 365 Document

Page Orientation implies to the direction in which a Word document is shown. Page Orientation in Word 365 are of two types, which are portrait (vertical arrangement) and landscape (horizontal arrangement). By default, Orientation in Word 365 is set at portrait.

To choose or change orientation, take these steps:

- Open the **Blank document** of your Word 365
- Click **Layout** tab

- Click **Orientation** which is under **Page Setup** category

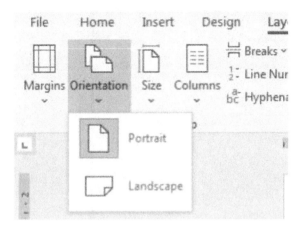

Fig 7.2: The two page Orientation types to choose from

- Click on any of the orientation types and that will be selected

How to change Document Size in Word 365

The **Size** tool under **Layout** tab is the button you need to change the size of documents you want to create using Word 365. By default, the documents size set in the Word application is **Letter** but you can change it by choosing from the preconfigured sizes or by creating a custom size.

To change the document size of Word 365 document, take these steps:

- Open a **Blank document** in your Word application
- Click Layout tab
- Click **Size** tool to see some options

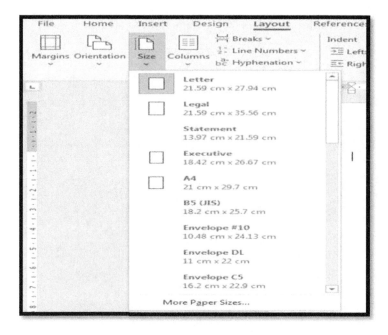

Fig 7.2: Changing document size in Progress

- Select any option from the list of sizes or click **More Paper Sizes...** and select the one you want

How to choose Columns Number

Depending on the kind of document style by column you want to have, you can use the document Column tool to make that possible. I know you have once seen some textbooks or other kinds of books that have texts written in a page of the book in two columns. Example of such books is the Holy books; Bible or Qur'an. So, you can create any number of columns in documents using Word 365 application.

To create columns in documents, take these steps:

- Open **Blank document** of Word 365
- Click the **Layout** tab
- Locate the **Columns** tool and click it

- From the options that will show up, select the number of columns you want to have in the document
- Start typing in your texts or if you have already typed your texts, the texts will be changed to the column number you chose.

Breaks under Layout tab in Page Setup Category

I have explained **Breaks** tool before now but let me still throw a little light again. **Breaks** tool performs two major tasks in Word document. The functions are to break documents into Pages and to divide documents into sections. When you click **Breaks**, you will be shown the options of whether you want to divide the pages of the document into pages or into sections. If you choose **Pages**, which is under **Page Break**, you will be taken to the next page. You can also break columns of a document and text wrapping. When you break a document having many pages into sections, you can have different sections and because of that can have different texts and numbers at the footer and header sections.

Line Numbers and Hyphenation Explained

These two tools in Word 365 are accessible under the **Layout** tab. The term **Hyphenation** implies the process of adding hyphens to words at the beginning of lines so the hyphenated part will fit at the end of the previous line. In this task, the hyphens are inserted between syllables in a word. **Hyphenation** can be done automatically or manually.

To use **Hyphenation** tool to insert hyphens in words, first click the **Layout** tab and then select **Hyphenation** tool. In the dialog box, choose either automatic Hyphenation or manual. Set you Hyphenation parameters and click **Ok**.

Line Numbers tool is used to add numbers to lines in a document. With this tool, Word 365 app can automatically count the lines in an entire document and display the appropriate number beside each line of text. In line numbering, a table inside that document is counted as one line. Also, text box and a figure is counted as one line each. To add line numbers to your entire document in Word 365, click the **Layout** tab and followed by **Line Numbers,** and then select **Continuous**.

The Paragraph Category of Insert Tab

The **Paragraph** tool of Word 365 under the **Layout** tab controls paragraph related tasks in Word document.

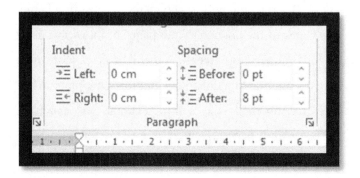

Fig 7.3: The **Paragraph** group under **Layout** tab

With the **Paragraph** tool, you can customize the paragraph section of any document you want to print out for use. All you are to do is to set the **Indent** and the **Spacing** sections to the standard you want them, and you are good to go. When you print the document from a printer, the parameters you set in the paragraph section before printing out the document is maintained.

Arrange Category of Layout Tab Explained

Arrange is one of the group tools under the **Layout** tab. With this tool, you can control how the objects in the Word document will appear. An example of an object as used here is picture. This group has its component tools as **Position, Wrap Text, Bring Forward, Send Backward, Selection Plane, Align, Group** and **Rotate.**

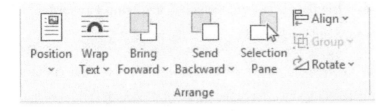

Fig 7.4: The **Arrange** group of **Layout** tab

With Position tool, you can set the picture to the position you want it. Just click on the picture, select **Layout** tab, and then click **Position** to select the way you want texts to wrap round the picture. You can position the picture with any form of text wrapping style. There are **Inline with Text position, Position in Top Center with Square Text Wrapping** and many others. Feel free to experiment with any of the position styles and see the result you will get.

How to apply Wrap Text in Word 365 Document
With the Wrap Text tool under Layout tab, you can choose how texts wrap around your selected object which can be a picture. To apply Wrap Text on or around any object, take these steps:

- As you have typed your texts and uploaded a photo or any other object in your document, click the **Layout** tab
- Click on the picture or any other object for it to be selected
- Click **Wrap Text** tool
- Select the wrap text style you want from the options

With the **Bring Forward** tool, you can bring your selected object forward one level or bring it in front of all other objects. If for instance I have about ten pictures in Word document, and I want an object that is last to come forward in front, I can use this tool to achieve it instead of copy and paste method. I am to select the picture and then click the **Bring Forward** tool. On the other hand, **Send Backward** tool does the reverse.

With **Selection Plane** tool, you can view the list of all the objects in a document. With this tool, you can see the order the objects are arranged and can also change the objects visibility. **Align** tool in **Arrange** category under **Layout** tab is used to change the placement of objects on a page in Word document. When you click on the object for example picture and then click **Align**, you will be shown some options on how to align the picture.

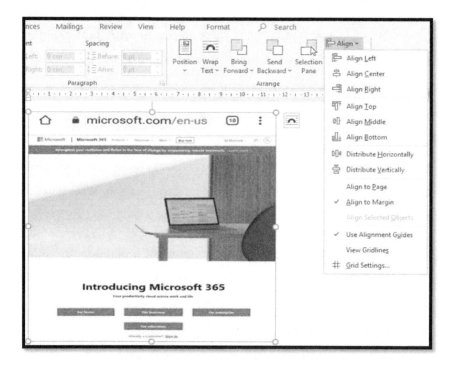

Fig 7.5: Options available in object **Align**

If for instance you select **Align Top** option, that picture will be taken to the top of that particular page. You can experiment with the other options and find out the change you will see.

How to rotate Images in Word 365

Some years back, I usually find it difficult to rotate images and other objects in Word application. In this section, I will teach you how to complete this task in Word 365.

To rotate images and objects in Word 365, take these steps:

- As you opened a document, click the **Layout** tab
- Click the image or picture you want to rotate
- Click the **Rotate** tool under the **Arrange** group
- Select the angle you want the image to be rotated to

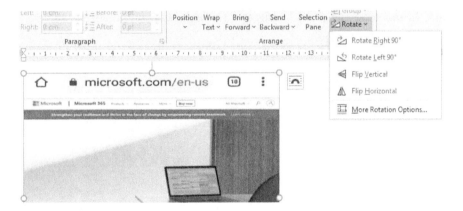

Fig 7.6: Image and object rotation options

You can click **More Rotation Options…** to customize your own rotation parameters. After, click the **Ok** button for it to take effect.

Chapter 8

Guide on Completing Some Tasks Through References Tab

There are many tasks you can complete through the **Reference** tab of Word 365. In this teaching, I will walk you through on that. But in all, they are about how to reference the paper works and articles you did or about to do. Let assume you have a book that you have written and want to arrange it and also reference the areas you sourced your information from, you can make it neat by making use of the tools available in the **References** tab.

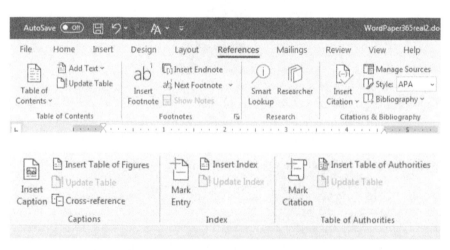

Fig 8: The Reference tab and the categories in it

From the above image, you see that there are some groups in the References tab. These groups are **Table of Contents**, **Footnotes**, **Research**, **Citation**

and Biography, and **Captions**. Through these groups, you can perform some tasks relating to their names.

How to Automatically Insert Table of Contents in Word 365 Document

There are many users of Microsoft Word that still insert table of contents in their documents manually without knowing that it can be done automatically. Word 365 is built with excellent tools that allows us to complete this task without stress.

To insert table of contents automatically in your document take these steps:

- Highlight each of the titles and subheadings texts that you want to have in your table of contents

If for example I have the chapter 1 of my book as "Introduction to Word 365" and have different subheadings in that chapter as well as other chapters and subheadings, I have to highlight them one by one.

- Click the **Home** tab of your document
- As you highlight each heading texts and subheadings, click the **Heading 1** or **Heading 2** tool which is one of the tools under the **Home** tab.

Make sure you do this for all the texts you want to add as contents of the book or article. Why you convert these titles and subheadings to headings is to remind Word 365 program that those are the parts you want to add to the table of contents. If you do not first convert them to headings, there is no how such titles and subheadings of your book or article can be added in the table of contents automatically. Also, when you click the **Heading 1** or **Heading 2** tool, you may lose some of your previous formatting on the texts like bold. What you have to do is to style the texts again. You can choose the font you want, font size and also make them bold again using the **bold** button in the Home tab.

- Click your computer cursor to any spot on the document where you want to list your table of contents
- Click the **References** tab
- Click **Table of Contents** tool

Fig 8.1: The options you will be shown when you select **Table of Contents** tool

- Click the **Automatic Table 1** option

Once you took the above steps, all the chapter/title texts and subheadings which you converted to headings previously will be added automatically as your book and articles table of contents. These are just the steps to take to insert table of contents automatically in Word 365.

Endnotes and How to Insert Them in Documents

An endnote is defined as a note printed at the end of a book or section of a book. In Word 365 document, endnotes are placed at the bottom of pages of the document. An endnote contains reference information about quoted material, example; *How to build a Website, Smart Books, 2020.*

To insert an endnote in a document, take these steps:

- Please your cursor on the last line of your document page where you want to insert endnote
- Click **References** tab at the top part of your Word environment
- Click **Insert Endnote** tool

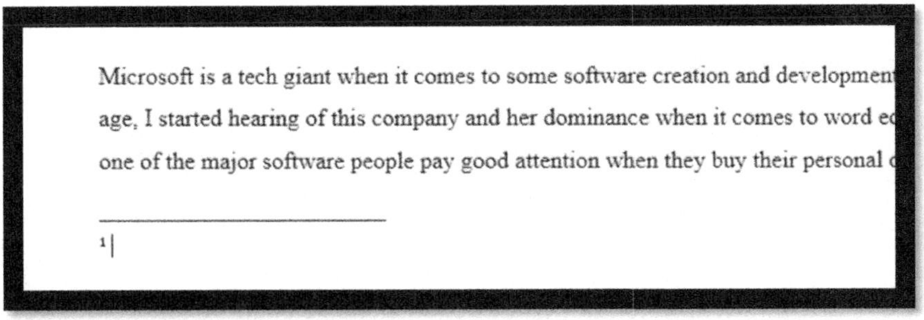

Microsoft is a tech giant when it comes to some software creation and development age, I started hearing of this company and her dominance when it comes to word e one of the major software people pay good attention when they buy their personal

1|

Fig 8.2: Endnote at the bottom of the page

- Write your endnotes texts

Looking at the picture above, you are to enter your endnote reference after the superscript "1". If I am to cite with the words I wrote before in the sample, I have to type *How to build a Website, Smart Books, 2020* after the superscripted "1".

Smart Lookup and Researcher Explained

Both **Smart Lookup** and **Researcher** are grouped under **Research** in Word 365. They are under References tab and are used to find further information on words, phrases and sentences. I sometimes call Word 365 a mini dictionary because of its Smart Lookup feature. With this property, you can find the meaning of words in a document without using a separate dictionary. But know that for the Smart Lookup to work, your computer must be connected to internet.

To find the meaning of words using Smart Lookup tool in Word 365, first highlight the word you want to find its meaning. The next is to click **References** tab, and then click **Smart Lookup** tool. Once you do this, you will be shown under **Explore** in detail about the word. Below is screenshot of the result I got when I searched for the word "software".

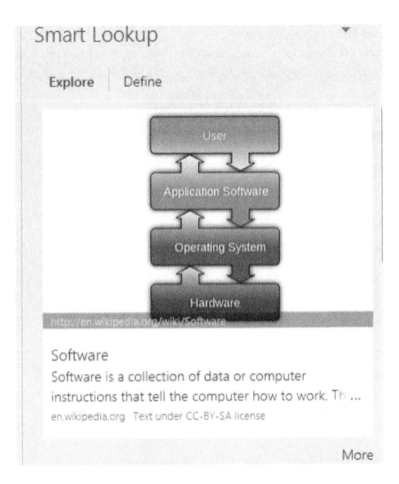

Fig 8.3: Look up tool in action

If you click **Define**, you will be given the meaning of the highlighted word.

Researcher tool is used to find out more information about a particular title in your document. It can help you find quotes, citable sources, and images. To see the power of this tool, just highlight the words or phrase which you want to get more information on, and then click **Researcher** tool. Know that this tool works with internet, and because of that your computer must be connected to the internet.

Citation and Biography Group

The **Citation and Biography** group covers everything you have to know about citation and biography in referencing. Say goodbye to trial and error once you understand how to make use of these tools.

Fig 8.4: The **Citation & Biography** group in **References** tab

A citation is a reference to a source of information you have in your document. It is inserted inside the body of a document to show the author you sourced a particular line of sentence or sentences from and the year of publication. In this context, a biography means a reference to a quoted source of information in a book or article involving mainly the author's name, the book or article title, date of publication, and the location the book was published. For you to use **Biography** tool effectively, you must have inserted that information in citation.

How to Insert Citation in Word 365 Document

To insert citation in document, take the following steps:

- Click the spot in the document where you want to insert the citation

Citation in most cases are inserted at the end of a sentence. So, if that is where you want to cite, just click the spot using your computer cursor.

- Click **References** tab at the top part of your Word app
- Click **Insert Citation** tool

When you click the **Insert Citation**, a new dialog box opens.

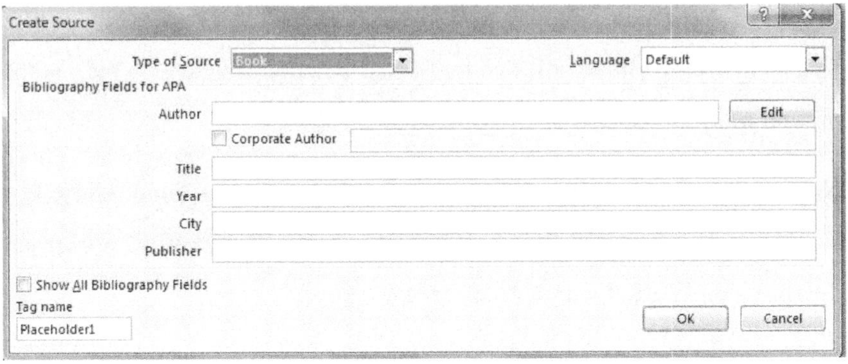

Create Source

Type of Source	Book	Language	Default

Bibliography Fields for APA

Author   [ ]   Edit

☐ Corporate Author

Title

Year

City

Publisher

☐ Show All Bibliography Fields

Tag name

Placeholder1   OK   Cancel

Fig 8.5: Setting up citation parameters

- Fill the information about the author or source which you want to cite

In the **Type of source**, select the type of source you want to cite. The work you want to cite may be Book, Website, Journal or any other form of document. Just select through the **Type of Source** line. In the above dialog box, I selected book. For **Author**, type the name of the author that wrote the book. If the book has Corporate author, just check the box. **Title** is where you should enter the title of the book. **Year** stands for the year of publication of the book. **City** implies the city where the book was published. And lastly, **Publisher** is where you are to type the name of the publishing company that published the book.

129

- When you are through with the filling of the parameters, just click the **Ok** button, and the citation will be inserted at that spot where you clicked to insert the citation at the beginning.

How to Insert Biography in Word 365

The biography is what we refer as reference section in books and project works. It usually appears at the last part of a project showing the authors name, title, year of publication, city and country. There are different referencing styles. But in this section, I will be choosing APA which is the most common.

Please note that you must have inserted citation before the **Biography**. It is the citation information that are used to build **Biography**. To insert biography in a Word document, take these steps:

- Click your cursor at a spot on any of the last pages of your document where you want the biography to be inserted
- Click **References** tab
- At **Style** under the **Citations & Biography** group, select the reference style you want to use, example APA
- Click **Biography** tool
- Select any of the biography options

Once you select any of the options, biography will be inserted on a part of the document where you want it.

The Captions and Index Groups

The **Captions** tools allow you to insert captions like figure numbers. Also, through this section, you can add **Table of Figures** in your document. For you to insert table of figures in your document successfully, you are to first insert caption, example numbering the images in your document first.

With the **Index** group, you can add index in your document. Instead of doing this manually, the Index tab makes it fast and easy for you. With the **Mark Entry**, you mark the keywords you want to have in your index section, which is usually at the last pages of the document. To mark any keywords, just highlight the word, click the **Mark Entry** tool, and then click **Mark** button of the dialog box. And with **Insert Index** tool, you insert those keywords you have marked as entry.

Step by Step Guide on Inserting Index Automatically in Word
To insert index at the last page of your document, just follow this step by step guide:

- Highlight the words or phrases you want the have in your index
- Click **References** tab and then click **Mark Entry** tool to see a dialog box as shown below:

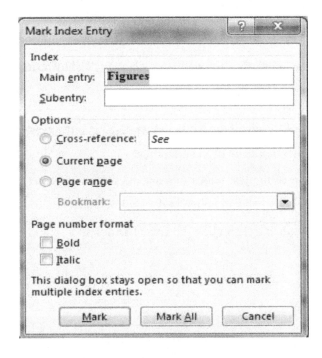

Fig 8.6: Mark Index Entry dialog box

In the **Main entry,** the word inside is **Figure** because I highlighted the word before I clicked **Mark Entry** tool. Leave **Subentry** empty unless you have any to add there. Under **Options**, select **Current page** as shown in the image. Under **Page number format**, you can leave the boxes empty or tick any if you want the words or keywords to be written in bold or italic when they appear on the index page.

- Click **Mark** or **Mark All** button

When you click **Mark,** only where the word appears on the page at that moment will be recorded when you finally insert index page in your document. But if you click **Mark All,** where that word or keywords appear in the entire document will be recorded by Word 365 system.

- Click **Close** to close the dialog box

When you click the **Close** button, you will notice that all the paragraph marks and hidden symbols in your document will be shown. To return the document to its normal state, click the **Home** tab, and then click **Show/Hide Paragraph** tool which takes the shape "¶".

- Repeat step 1, 2, 3, 4 to add all the word, keywords, and phrases you want to have in the index page of the document
- Scroll down to one of the last pages of your document where you want to insert the index page and click at the spot.
- Click **References** tab and then click the **Insert Index** tool to show dialog box below:

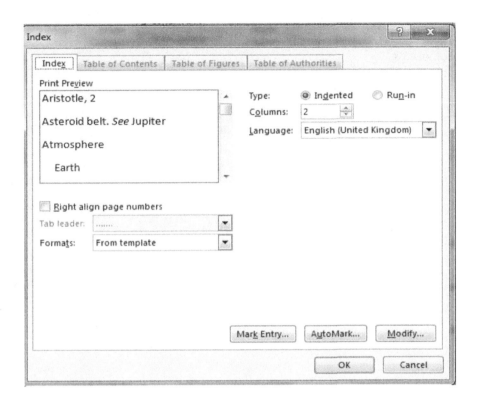

Fig 8.7: Insert Index dialog box

In the **Formats**, you can click the dropdown to choose the format you want. As you choose the format, you will see the sample of how the index will look like in the **Print Preview**.

- Click **Ok** button for the index to be inserted

Table of Authorities Explained

Table of Authorities is defined as a list of all of the sources cited in a legal document that notes the page numbers on which each source has been cited. To insert table of authorities, you have to first mark the citation, and **Mark Citation** tool will help you to do that. So, select the texts first and then click **Mark Citation** for the texts to be added as what will be added in table of authorities. When you click the **Insert Table of Authorities** tool after marking all the citations, the marked texts will be added in the table of authorities.

Chapter 9

Mailings and Review Explained

In this chapter, I will walk you through to understand the tasks you can complete using the **Mailings** and the **Review** tabs which are available in Word 365 interface. The **Mailings** tab covers sending and preparing your documents for mailing purpose. On the other hand, the **Review** tab has to do with checking the documents and the texts you have on it to make sure everything is in order.

Completing Basic Tasks Through Mailings Tab of Word 365

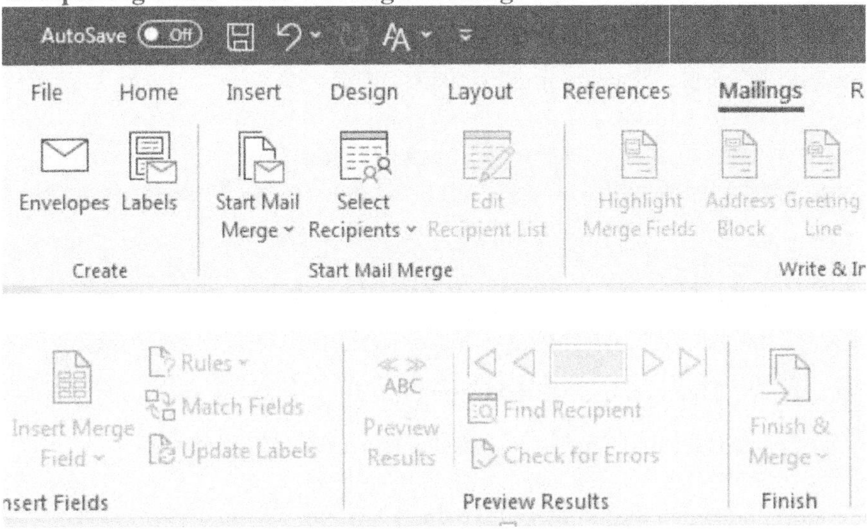

Fig 9: The screenshot of the Mailing tab

The above image is the screenshot of the Mailing tab of Word 365. The tab is grouped into categories. These are Create, Start Mail Merge, Write & Insert Fields, Preview Results, and Finish. You will find out that some of the categories are disabled at default, example, the Write and Insert Fields. The Write & Insert Fields section of the Mailings tab of the ribbon for instance is disabled by default. The controls in that section will only be enabled when the active document is a mail merge main document with a data source attached to it. So, once this standard is met, it will be enabled.

Envelopes and Labels

The above two are under the Create group of Mailings tab. With **Envelopes** and **Labels** tools, you can create the envelope you want to use to send the mails physically. You can create the size of the envelope you want to send the mail with, and the address you want to have as a delivery address. Click the individual tools and insert the information expected from you. After entering the required data, you can click **Print** to print out the envelope containing the information entered. Note that these tools are used to create envelopes for physical sending of mails.

Mail Merge and the use in Word 365

With **Mail Merge** tool, you can send mass mail to many recipients within a short time. If for example you have a company and have customer base of about twenty thousand, do you think it will be convenient for you to be sent mail to them individually when what you want to do is to send the mail to all at once? That is what **Mail Merge** does for you. With this tool, you can customize a mail and send it out at once to all your customers.

To start and finish mail merge, take these steps:

- Click the **Mailings** tab of your document
- Click **Start Mail Merge** tool

- Choose the type of document you want to use to deliver the mail

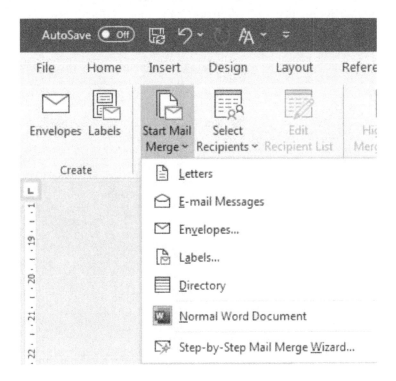

Fig 9.1: Choose the type of document you want to use to create mail from the list

- Type in the body of your mail.

Just type in the body of the mail you will like to send out to the masses. Do not type the recipients address and the greetings or solution section. We will set them up using the **Mailings** tools as we make progress. Just follow my guide.

- Click **Select Recipients** tool
- From the options, you can select **Type a New List** (when you do not have your list of recipients prepared already), **Use an Existing List** (When have a soft copy document containing all the lists of your

recipients), or **Choose from Outlook Contacts** (when you want to source your recipients from Microsoft's Outlook application).

- If you choose **Type a New List** option, then type in the detail of the recipients one by one as in the dialog box as shown in the image below:

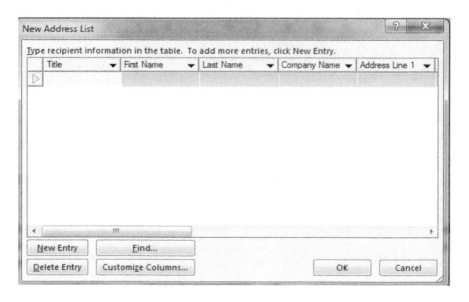

Fig 9.2: Fill in the data for the recipient

From the above picture, after typing one customer's contact details, click **New Entry** button to add another person's detail. Try and fill the basic information because the required information is much by default. Continue this process until you are done with all the recipients details you want to add.

- Click **Ok** button to save your recipients details
- The above action will open a folder in your computer to save the file containing your recipients detail. You can choose to save the file in any location in your computer. Once you do so, the tool in **Write & Insert Fields** become activated as well as other disabled tools at start.

- Click **Address Block** tool to add address

The **Address Block** tool is there to help you add address to your letter. Choose what you want to be included in your recipients letter. Uncheck any part of the address you do not want to be added. Click **Ok** for the place to add address to be placed inside your document.

- Type in the address of your company or business in the place with the texts "**AddressBlock**". Delete the texts and add your company or business address.
- Take you cursor down after adding the address block and click at a spot
- Click **Greeting Line** tool for you to choose the greetings your recipients will see in the mail

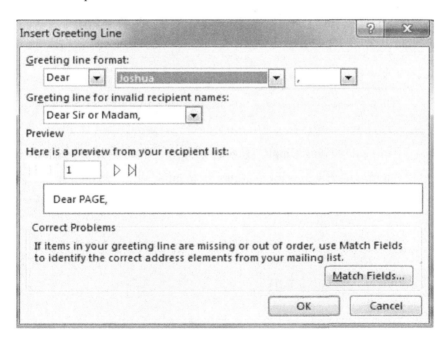

Fig 9.3: Setting up greeting line which your recipients will see when the mails are sent

In the **Greeting line format**, just choose the format you want. If the recipients involve both males and females, I recommend you choose only the name option as shown in the image. In the **Greeting line for invalid recipient names**, choose any option of your choice as well. Click **Ok** to save your information after making your choice.

- Click **Insert Merge Field** tool to add some information like Last names, company names or phone numbers of your recipients.
- Click **Preview Results** tool to see how your recipients will receive their mails.

You can use the arrow symbol under the **Preview Results** to see how each recipient will receive his or her mail. If you do not like the way it appears, go to the appropriate tool in that **Mailings** tab and make the change you want to see. You can delete any part of the mail merge you do not want to see inside the document, and it will be updated in the Word system.

- Click **Finish and Merge** tool and select **Print Documents** option when you are sure everything is fine the way they appeared in the **Preview Results** stage. If you want to send them out as email, you can select **Send Email Messages** option and fill in the expected data. Also, if you want to edit individual documents, then select the option for it.

LOVE KELVIN

NANA TUGS

NO 22 THREE STREET

CALIFORNIA

Dear MR KELVIN,

We at Smart Prints write to wish you merry Christmas. We are happy you made it to this point irrespective of all the difficulties we passed through this year due to the pandemic. We are happy to have you as one of our great customers.

You are important to us and continue to keep safe.

Smart Prints USA

Merry Christmas

Fig 9.4: A copy of the document to be sent to one of my recipients

The Review Tab

In this section of this chapter, I will guide you through on some tasks you can complete through Review tab. As earlier said, the Review ribbon contains more of how to check some information you have in your Word document.

Fig 9.5: The Review tab and the component tools

Check your Grammar and Spelling

To check your grammar and spelling after typing in the Word document, take these few steps:

- Click the **Review** tab at the top part of your Word interface
- Click the **Spelling & Grammar** tool

When you click that tool, it will show you some spellings and grammar that may not be correct in the document. You are to decide whether to accept the correct spelling and grammar suggested by the Word system or not.

Thesaurus

The word thesaurus implies another closely related word to a word. With the **Thesaurus** tool, you will find another word close a particular word by meaning. Example, the thesaurus to the word "important" is significant, vital and central.

To use the **Thesaurus** tool, just highlight the word and click the **Thesaurus** tool which is under **Review** tab. This will show you the result by the right-hand margin of your Word environment.

Checking your Word Count

It is important to check the word count of the texts you have in your document. To achieve this, take these steps:

- Click the **Review** tab
- Click **Word Count** tool and that will show you the number of words in the document.

Use of Read Aloud Tool

The **Read Aloud** is a tool under Review tab that you can use to instruct Word 365 application to read the words in a document to your hearing or to the hearing of people close to your computer. The spot you click your cursor is where the **Read Aloud** will start reading the words in your document. And if you want it to stop reading when it gets to a point, click on the Read Aloud tool to stop reading.

To use the tool, take these steps:

- With your cursor, click at a spot in your document where you want it to start reading
- Click **Review** tab
- Click **Read Aloud**

Accessibility Check
This tool which is in Review tab is used to check if your document follows the accessibility best practice. When you click the tool, it will run through your document and informs you if your document follows accessibility best practice or not.

Use of Translate
You can use **Translate** tool to translate a language to another in Word 365. You are to make sure that your computer is connected to the internet for you to successfully translate from one language to another. When you are using this tool for the first time, it may take time before the words are translated to another language.

To translate from one language to another, take these steps:

- Highlight the word or words you want to translate
- Click **Review** tab
- Click **Translate** tool and select **Translate selection** option

The selected words are translated, and the result shown to you by the margin at the right.

Chapter 10

Reading and Getting Word Help

In this chapter, I will guide you through on how you can view you Word documents in different ways. This depends on what you want to do with the document contents which can be texts and pictures at that point in time. The different ways through which you can view your documents are available in the **View** tab of Word 365. Also, I will guide you on how you can get help from Microsoft Corporation if anything goes wrong as you enjoy your Word 365 package. I will go extra mile to cover other areas of the word processing software which I know will be important to you.

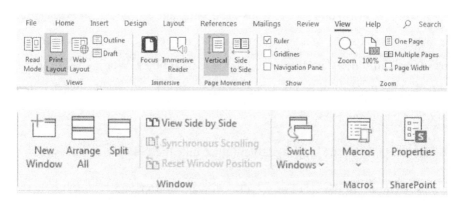

Fig 10.1: The tools available in the View tab of Word 365

Switching to Reading Mode

The Reading Mode is the best mode to read texts on your screen. It gives you clear view of the words you have typed on the Word environment and makes editing easy. If you are done writing all the texts in your document and want to proofread, it is recommended you switch to reading mode with the tool. To switch to reading mode take these steps:

- Click the **View** tab of your Word 365 application
- Click **Reading Mode** tool

To exit **Reading Mode**, just press the escape button of your computer keyboard. The escape button has the letter **esc** written on it and it appears at the top right-hand corner of most Windows computers.

Viewing your Document in Print Mode

The Print Layout is the default mode of document in Word 365. In that regards, when you are typing texts on your Word app, the software is already programmed to be in that mode. If you send your document at that point to printer, the document will be printed the way it appears in your computer screen which is the A4 paper size. To confirm that your document is in the Print Layout Mode, just click **View** tab of Word 365 and you will see that the **Print Layout** tool is already selected.

Knowing how your Document Appears on the Web

The way your document appears on your Word screen is not the same it will appear on the internet. The settings of the two are quite different. If you want to know how your document will appear on the web when the texts are copied and then posted in a website, take these steps:

- Click the **View** tab
- Select **Web Layout** tool and you will see how it will be on the web.

If you want to exit Web Layout mode, just press the escape (esc) button of your computer keyboard.

Outline and Draft Tools Explained

With **Outline** tool, you can see your content in outline form. In this situation your document is shown as bulleted points. The usefulness of this view is that it helps in creating headings and moving the whole paragraphs in a document.

To view your document in outline form, take these steps:

- Click the **View** tab of your Word
- Click the **Outline** tool

Immediately you take the above step, the texts in your document will be shown to you in the outline mode. To exit your document from **Outline** view, click the **Close Outline View** button.

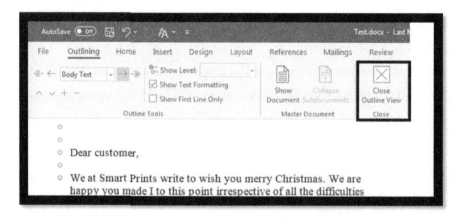

Fig 10.2: The **Close Outline View** button identified in the picture

On the other hand, **Draft tool** is another tool you can select to view your document differently. This tool allows you to view only the texts in your document. It also makes editing your work easy. If you switch to **Draft** view and there were other objects in the document before the switch example images, the objects will not be shown. But when you switch back to normal Print Layout mode, your pictures are restored back to their rightful positions. Also, Draft view hides headers and footers sections of a document.

Take these steps to view documents in **Draft** mode

- Click **View** tab
- Click **Draft** tool

To move back to the normal Print Layout mode, just click the **Print Layout** tool

Viewing your Document in Focus and Immersive Reader

Microsoft makes it possible by leaving you with many options on how you want to view your documents. **Focus** mode as the name implies is newly integrated into Word 365 to make you focus as you read through your documents and avoid any form of distraction that may pop-up on your computer screen. When you change to Focus view, your document covers your entire computer screen and all you see is your document contents like texts and images.

These are the steps you need to take to switch your document to Focus view:

- Click **View** tab
- Click **Focus** tool

Immediately you click the **Focus** tool, your document will be switched to that mode. Anytime you want to exit Focus view, just click the escape (esc) key on your computer keyboard.

You can use the **Immersive Reader** tool to improve your reading skill. In this mode, you can adjust how text in your document is displayed and can also make the texts in your document read aloud to your hearing. When your document is in Immersive mode, you can select **Syllables** tool to see the syllables in each word in your document. If you want to switch to Immersive Reader, just click **View** tab followed by **Immersive Reader** tool. When you are done viewing your document in that mode and want to exit, click **Close Immersive Reader**.

Switching Document to Slide to Slide

You can choose to see the whole pages of your document using **Slide to Slide** tool. When your document is changed to this mode, you can scroll through the pages through the bottom part of Word screen. You can slide the pages from right to left or from left to right.

To enable the slide by slide feature, take these few steps:

- Click the **View** tab of the document
- Click **Slide to Slide** tool

Immediately you took the last step, your document will be switched to slide to slide. If you want to exit from this view mode, just click **Vertical** tool, and it will go back to its original state.

Zooming Your Document

The term "zoom" in Microsoft Word means to increase or decrease the size of the document that appears on your Word screen. You may like to zoom your document to the level you want it. By default, Word 365 documents are placed on 100% zoom level but you can choose your own zoom level. There are two ways you can zoom your document.

You can quickly zoom your document by taking your cursor down to the bottom right margin part of your screen and then click the **100%** zoom level.

Fig 10.3: The **100%** zoom level position shown by the arrow

When you click the **100%** zoom level, it will open a new dialog box where you can choose the zoom level you want.

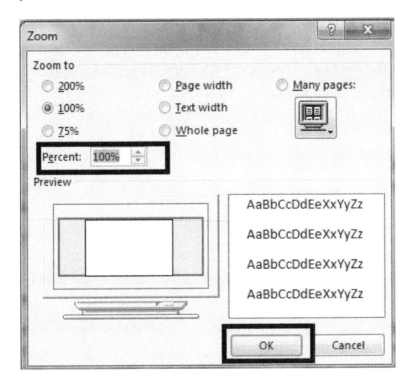

Fig 10.4: The Zoom level dialog box

From the dialog box, you can set your parameters. In the **Percent**, you can type the percentage level you want your document to be zoomed to or use the up or down arrow to control that. When you are done, just click the **Ok** button for you to see the change appear in your document.

Zooming your document through View tab

Another way you can zoom your document is through the **View** tab of your Word 365 app. To zoom your document through your **View** tab, take these steps:

- Click **View** tab
- Click **Zoom** tool
- Insert your parameters
- Click **Ok** button

New Window Explained

With New Window tool, you can open a document in another window. With this property, you can work in different palaces at the same time.

To open your document in new window, take these steps:

- Click **View** tab
- Click **New Window** tool

As you took the last step, that same document you are working on will be opened in another window of your Word 365 application. If you want to see these two documents appear on your same screen, click the **View Side by Side** tool. By doing so, when you make changes in one document, you can quickly do that in the other one. If you want to exit that **View Side by Side** mode, just click the same **View Side by Side** tool and you will see only one document on your screen.

Understanding the Help Tab

The **Help** tab is an added feature when compared to the other old versions of Microsoft Word.

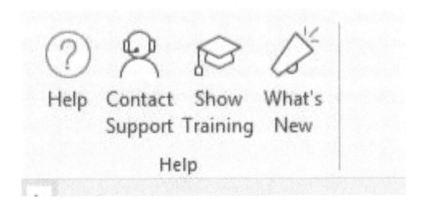

Fig 10. 5: The commands available in **Help** tab

The tools/commands available in the **Help** tab are **Help, Contact Support, Show Training**, and **What's New.** Your computer must be connected to internet before you can use any of these tools. To access Help commands, just click the **Help** tab. With these tools, you can get help from Microsoft if you run into technical issue or want to know more about some tools in the Word app. Take for instance you want to reach the Microsoft Word 365 customer service, you can click **Contact Support** tool, and then reach out to them.

The Search Box
The search box is located by the right after the **Help** tab.

Fig 10. 6: The Search Box of Word 365

With the Search, you can type in any tool name you want to find, and suggestions will be shown to you. From the suggestions, you can select any tool that is close to what you are searching for. Take for instance I want to find page numbering tool, and do not know how to locate it, I can start typing "page number" in the **Search**, and some options will show up as I type in the texts that makes up the words. I will then select any from the options and complete my action.

Sharing Your Document with Others

After you have written all the texts you want to have in your document, you may like to share the document with your team of workers or other people. You can share the document with them right from the Word 365 environment. You can share the document in either Word Document format or in PDF format.

To share the document which you created using Word 365, take these steps:

- Click the **Share** by the top right-hand corner of your Word interface

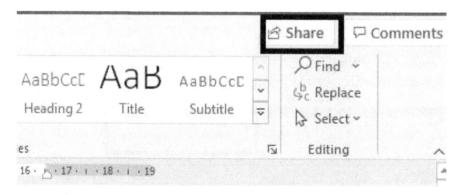

Fig 10.7: The **Share** tool indicated in the picture

- Chose the format you want to share the document

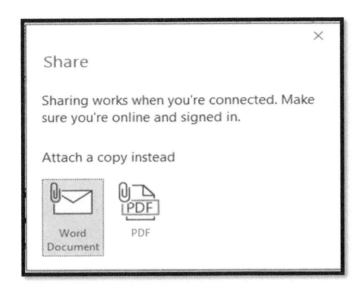

Fig 10.8: Select any of the two document share options

You can choose to share the document in Word Document format or PDF

- Set up an Outlook account if requested from you
- Enter the email addresses of the recipients and send the document to them.

Finding Texts in Word 365 Document
The **Find** tool located at the top right side of Word interface under Share tool is used to find words in a document. You may like to find words in document because you want to make correction or for any reason best known to you.

To find words in a document, take these steps

- Click **Home** tab

- Click the **Find** tool of your Word 365

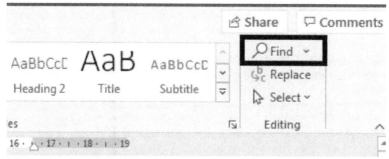

Fig 10.9: The **Find** tool shown

- Type in the words, phrases or clauses you want to search
- If the words are available in the document, you will be shown where they appear in your document.
- Use the up or down arrow to locate the exact location of the words

Working on Images in your Document

There are some actions you can take on images you inserted in your Word document. You can copy the images, cut, crop or resize the images.

To perform any of those tasks, just right-click on the picture and you will see some options as shown below:

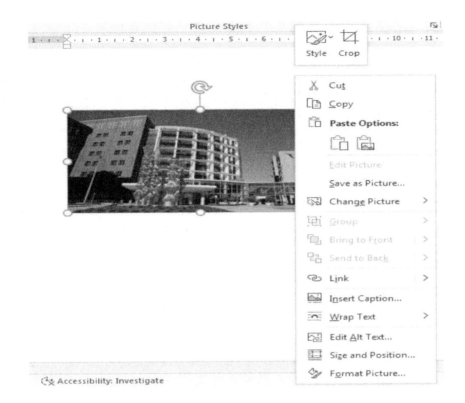

Fig 10.1.1: An image and options available when I right clicked the image

If you want to crop the image, click **crop** and adjust the cropping to the level you want it on the picture. When you have adjusted the picture to your taste, just click out of the picture.

If you want to cut the picture, just click **cut**

If you want to copy the picture, just click **Copy**.

Also, if you want to save the picture in your computer or OneDrive, just click **Save as Picture**, and select the location you want to save the picture.

To resize the picture, just click **Size and Position** after right-clicking on the picture. This will open a dialog box for you. In the **Height,** which is a part in the dialog box, increase or reduce the Percent depending on whether you want to increase or reduce the size of the image. Click **Ok** button when you are done setting your parameters.

How to Compress Images in Word 365 Document

Sometimes you may not like to have your file size big because of what you want to use the file for. On the other hand, images/pictures make file size big. To reduce the size of the document, that is where the need to compress images come in. If you want to compress all the images in the entire document, you can do that through one of the pictures in the document.

To compress images, take these steps:

- Click on an image in the document

Sometimes, immediately you click on the image, some image tools show on the top part of the Word toolbar section but if they do not show up, continue with these steps:

- Click **Format** which will appear on top part of the Word tab section

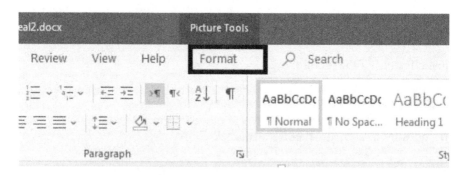

Fig 10.1.2: Format tool indicated

- Click **Compress Pictures** icon

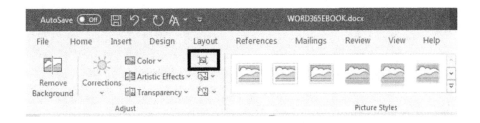

Fig 10.1.3: **Compress Pictures** icon indicated

- In the dialog box that will show up, set how you want the picture to
  be compressed

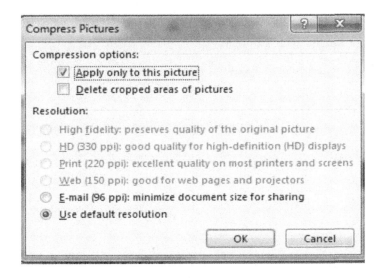

Fig 10.1.3: Dialog box to set image compression parameters

If you want the compression to apply to all the pictures in the entire
document, uncheck the box at **Apply only to this picture**. If you want all
the cropped areas in your pictures to be removed, then check the box **Delete
cropped areas of pictures**. I advise you select the **Use default resolution**
as it is by default.

- Click **Ok** button for the pictures to be compressed

Appreciation and Contact Channel

My Appreciation

Thanks for reading

Contact Me

You can reach me through my email address: customersbase2019@gmail.com

Index

Printed in Great Britain
by Amazon